IN A SMALL HOUSE
ON THE
OUTSKIRTS OF HEAVEN

In a Small House on the Outskirts of Heaven

Tom Wayman

HARBOUR PUBLISHING

HARBOUR PUBLISHING CO. LTD.
P.O. Box 219
Madeira Park, BC
V0N 2H0

Cover design & illustration by Roger Handling

Printed & bound in Canada

CANADIAN CATALOGUING IN PUBLICATION DATA

Wayman, Tom, 1945 –
   In a small house on the outskirts of heaven

   Poems.
   ISBN 1-55017-002-3

   I. Title
PS8595.A915 1989   C811'.54   C89-091009-X
PR9199.3.W3915 1989

■ CONTENTS

◼ TESTIMONIES

ONE LUMP OR TWO

In your sugar bowl, *Frank said*,
sugar gets hard and sticks to the sides.
It's no different in the various silos
at the Spreckels mill.
Three of us are lowered on ropes
into a silo each shift,
dressed in a sort of moon suit
with pickaxe and shovel.
For the next eight
we pry the sugar from the walls.

Each time when I touched bottom
I'd say to myself: "It's a small step
for a man, but a giant leap
for the working class." The foreman
never went down. He's supposed to stay on top
to watch our ropes
but he regularly takes off somewhere.
Anyway, nobody bothers to be hauled up
when we have to take a piss.
We just let fly where we stand.
I stopped using sugar much when I got that work.

They had us on rotating shifts
which I didn't like.
But graveyards were best.
I or somebody would carve a bed
in the sugar, out of the foreman's line of vision.
We'd usually manage
to each grab a few hours sleep during the night.

Strangest part of the job, though,
was my boots. No matter how clean they looked
when I took them off
or where in the house I left them
they'd both be completely covered with ants
when I'd go to put them on for work again.

■ IT'S AN IMPOSSIBLE SITUATION

Laura said. You're supposed to dress well
yet you don't earn enough
to buy good clothes and also live decently.
They want you to be friendly and charming
but not forward. Feminine,
but if they chase you around the desk
it's your fault: you led them on.
You're supposed to have the brains
to understand where everything belongs, how it works,
what is happening and why
yet not be so smart they
have to pay you for what you know.

                                        It's not surprising

so many secretaries are snappy
with people, peculiar,
half crazy. I had to quit before I
was that way too.

■ COST PLUS

Working for cost-plus contractors,
Dave said, is the pits.
One site I was on the company told us:
"Show up sick, drunk, we don't care.
Just don't miss a shift."
It was all money in their pockets.

This was constructing the methanol refinery
at Kitimat. The company's deal with the owners
gave an extra week to complete the job
for each day of any labor stoppage,
which meant the company would rake in even more.
So they kept trying to get us to wildcat.
They would tell the Teamsters, for example,
the drivers no longer could have
their half-hour safety inspection each morning.
Naturally, the drivers pulled a wobble
and there went a day. Next the company would announce

something similar
and another trade would pack it in.

The worst incident involved an electrical conduit
crossing the site underground.
A guy with a backhoe was digging
and hit it: blew the seals right out of his machine
and scared the crap out of him.
We asked for a blueprint
of where the cable was laid.
But the company refused. Said they had no idea
where the cable was, and so on. We downed tools.
After about a week, with all that money
stacked up, the company
suddenly produces the chart
and work starts again.
They could have had that blueprint in our hands
two minutes after the acccident.
But here the company is laughing
all the way to the bank
and issuing statements to the media
about the rotten labor climate in this province.

Eventually we got tired of this scam
being used against us. Somebody found
the company wouldn't receive more time on their contract
if a stoppage was a Compensation Board matter.
Now, Compo regulations for cranes
say we have the right to inspect the boom
before each lift. And that's what we did.
We would hoist a toolbox five stories up to the roof,
then bring the boom to the ground
and for the next couple of hours examine thoroughly
the sheaves, cable, even the welds on the boom tubing.
Then we would lift a sling of lumber
and down the boom would come
for another two or three hour inspection.
The company was going nuts
but after a day or so they caught on
and stopped provoking walkouts
and let us build.

■ THE BIG THEFT
for Howard White

It's one of those myths
from the workplace, told by somebody who is sure
the story is true. So you believe it, until

you find yourself listening to another version
of the tale. In this case
let's call it The Big Theft. I first heard it
in a truck assembly plant:

before you came, Tom, there was a guy,
Roger Hutchison, worked here:
an oldtimer. The guard caught him
at the gate one afternoon
leaving with an oil pressure gauge in his lunchkit.
Hell, we all take something home
if we can use it—clips or seat cushions—
Roger was just unlucky and got nabbed.
But for some reason they went around to his house
and discovered a nearly-completed truck
in his garage. Over the years, he had boosted
piece by piece almost everything for it.
He'd obviously gotten help moving the larger items
like the frame or the engine
from the parts yard. But he had built
pretty damn close to an entire tractor unit
in his spare time.

                    Then at coffee
on a renovation job:
Donny used to be employed at a brickworks
where a man each day
took a brick home in his lunchbox.
Only one brick. But when the man dropped dead of a heart attack
the week before he was due to retire
they found he had stockpiled
a few bricks less than the total he needed
to construct his dream house.

How this myth began isn't hard to grasp.
Even the dullest among us can understand
no amount of money the company pays
really compensates for the time and effort
the job takes out of our lives.
As the slogan says: *the things we give up*
to go to work
are never returned. It's pleasant to imagine
some person someplace turning the tables.

And as with every myth, there's a lesson here.
This teaches we can gain possession
of what we make where we are employed
but not by acting alone.

Plus, it is evident
rent-a-cops aren't posted at the office door at quitting time
to check the executives' briefcases
or certain envelopes addressed to the owners.
If these containers were opened
inside would be revealed
part of the value of the labor we perform each shift
being snuck out past the fence.
What these people remove secretly
isn't material required on this job
so they don't consider their actions stealing.
Yet from our work
a group of men and women get richer than us
without even asking us to vote
on whether we consent to this situation.
And that's
no myth.

■ WHY PART-TIME STAFF DON'T RECEIVE
PRORATED BENEFITS
for Jack Finnbogason

We don't require people. Instead,
we identify specific functions to be performed.
Consider a sessional: employed, say,

to teach geography. We can use her throat
where the vocal cords are, but not her teeth.
Why should we pay part of a dental plan?
If I purchase a chalkboard from a dealer
I don't also have to buy a desk they're offering for sale.

You argue that because someone
has a clerical job with us six hours a day
we should contribute six-eighths of
his or her medical premiums. But these employees
have complete use of their bodies
for the eighteen hours a day we have absolutely no control
over what they do.
Rather than extend coverage to part-time help
our immediate goal in negotiations is to reduce
payment of full-time employees' benefits
to a fairer level: from one hundred per cent
to eight twenty-fourths.
You can see how reasonable this is.
Whatever damage the staff cause to their health
during their hours off work
should be their responsibility.
I hope you'll agree, too, this is merely a first step
toward establishing a more equitable arrangement.
Next we intend to calculate
how many days each month an employee isn't present
—sick time, weekends and holidays, for instance—
and take these into account
in determining our share of coverage.

That is what we should be discussing
when we talk about prorated benefits.
Such a change makes better use
of the institution's financial and human resources.
Don't we both want this? To minimize expenses
while spending the dollars we have most efficiently?
Which is why our plan for the long term
is to hire the majority of non-managerial personnel
only for certain targeted skills.
This policy allows for more flexibility
in meeting the demands of the market.

We must realize the era of the full-time employee
—except for executives—has passed.
And if the part-timers object to
the thrust of our current operational strategy
they should remember: individuals like them
have just a casual involvement here.
Believe me, those of us with a total commitment to this place
understand best what it needs.

■ THE GATES

There are wire gates and glass doors
in my city
that are portals which lead back
to another time.

If we cross through, we revert to an era
before people such as ourselves won the right to vote.
Inside this zone
where most of us must stay eight hours daily,
we are expected to memorize the reasons
why orders of our superiors
have to be obeyed.
We learn if the democracy that is praised
in the century we have travelled from
were applied here
the consequence would be inefficiency.
Yet, in our breaks, testimonials to the waste
of hours, materials, and human effort
are a staple of our talk.
Meanwhile, the cash which the owners
have put into this enterprise
is also offered as a justification
of others' right to command.
But is money
more important than democracy?
In the period to which we return after work
are only the richest
permitted to vote? And aren't our lives
—shaped and bent to fit this job—
of value?

If the owner could run this enterprise alone
he or she would. The moment another human being
is hired, don't two people work here?
Since two are now involved
why shouldn't both decide how to perform the job?
Forget it, authorities tell us,
the boss knows more than you.
But who declared skills
equivalent to power?
Left to ourselves, you show me
what has to be accomplished
and I, you, according to need
without a hierarchy of supervision.

Indeed, after the shift
we pass to a date where we are considered equal citizens
of a community. Not until hours later
do we stand once more on the brink
of the previous time, waiting for the buzzer
which suspends for another day our liberty.

And such shuttling back and forth
can be dangerous.
When, inside the portals, we express certain beliefs
commonly accepted centuries later
we are branded a heretic or blasphemer
—serious crimes, in this earlier period.
Or, unfortunate ideas that belong to the past
get transported by some of us into today.

If the situation were the plot of a science fiction yarn
a hero or heroine would remedy the problem
by cutting off the power to the gates,
releasing everyone from their bizarre enslavement.
In real life, I think,
there isn't any mechanical solution.
Rather, we each have to help push
the world we inhabit while we are employed
forward to the present and beyond,

before this schizophrenia of
living half obedient and half free
confuses us completely.

■ UNEMPLOYED

> "Unemployment is not a disease.
> It has no cure."
> —slogan, 1980s

Being without work is not a sickness
Yet those of us affected

have been given symptoms
The source of these

is the statement:
there are jobs for all

*and if you don't have one
you are ill*

stupid, a loser
Instead of agreeing together

what work is necessary, decent
worth accomplishing

and that everyone alive, employed or not
has needs we must see met

we are handed a slip of paper
marked *infected*

on which is also printed
it is your responsibility

*now you are sick
to cure yourself*

This paper has to be eaten
every two weeks

But the stomach
cannot dissolve the paper entirely

Undigested shreds
mat in your guts

and an animal spawns there
The animal weighs down our intestines

hurts our organs when it rises
on its legs to shift position

sends its breath up
into ours

Now we feel weak
Now we can pound and pound

on the roof of the station wagon
yell in the bar about

shooting the welfare minister
But it is your child you slap

his head jerking sideways
as the blow connects

It is your wife, or another woman
whose face you turn into meat

Yet this is not a disease
it is a decision:

this is how we want
our citizens to live

A decision
does not have a cure

It remains in effect
until another choice is made

But if the decision is left
to those who benefit from the situation

this might go on for years
—whatever someone else promises

before we vote for them
again

These say: *if you elect me*
you can stop eating that paper

The animal
will disappear

Not one says: *if I am elected, nobody*
will have to eat the paper

Even if they did speak this, they would lie
because the decision was not made

in an election
and cannot be reversed by that procedure

But there are
methods

There is
another way

■   TIES
      for Judy Wapp and David Everest

If you look closely at those who speak about
''our flag'' or ''our country''
you'll observe they have one thing in common:
they wear ties. In each sector of the globe
this is the same: before they get you to kill
for them, or suffer for them, or hate for them
they put on a tie, pick up the speech
somebody else was paid to write, step to

12

a microphone and start. Ties
are the real flags of such people.
The few women or priests among them dress
in an equally recognizable manner.
But ties let them identify their counterparts
in different geographic areas.
Later, after the war
or the crisis or the trade dispute
it will be revealed that the men and women of the ties
made lots of money through deals in the other region
while they were buying and selling
the lives of the rest of us
or the products we create at work
or the minerals or crops found locally.
Then the ties begin to flap
about the ''natural historic friendship
between our two great peoples''
until the time comes to seal a border again,
recall ambassadors
and energetically wave the flags.
But always the first allegiance
these talkers pledge to in the morning
is their ties.

On the plaza at the United Nations building in New York
instead of flagpole after flagpole displaying
the massed banners of the globe
they should run up the world's ties:
board of director ties,
central committee ties,
senior administrative staff ties.
This would give a more accurate picture
to the tours of school kids or anyone else attempting to grasp
what goes on around the planet.

Or, every household,
each family could fly their own flag.
Every group or organization so inclined.
Some would be more elaborate than others,
some especially imaginative. All sorts of devices,
slogans, shapes, trim.

Under such circumstances, if a tie so much as breathes
the word ''fatherland'' or ''motherland''
the evidence will be visible to everybody:
we are many, not one. Individuals, not a herd.
Differences, solidarities, uniquenesses.
And we might choose
other groupings than at present.
A majority of flags could even decide
to end the tieocracy,
the rule by these treacherous little
scraps of cloth.

■ A CURSING POEM: THIS POEM WANTS GORDON
SHRUM TO DIE
1971

This poem wants to hurt another person.
This poem wants another person to die.
It wants him to suddenly stumble
feel a sharp pain just under the belly
a harsh pain, one that rips him so hard inside that he shits
        himself.
The poem wants him to become dizzy
feel a rush of sweat on the face
to begin to shiver, and have to be helped into bed.
The poem wants his teeth to chatter, wants him to throw up
gasping for air, wants mucus to pour from his nose and mouth.
It wants him to die in the night.

This poem wants Gordon Shrum to die.
First because despite all his company's rules and tariffs
despite every regulation they tell the press they apply
his company turned off the heat and light in the house.
They did this without warning, when the temperature was forty
        degrees by day
and the nights begin at four o'clock.
So that after working all day, the body could come home
to a room of black ice.

So after straining all day at the jobsite, with the fingers
numb at the hammer and slipping under the weight of the heavy
     boards
after the back was twisted trying to hoist the load of a
     wheelbarrow
the rest of the body could return to darkness and cold.

This poem also wants Gordon Shrum to die
because his company charges twenty-five cents every day
for the bus to carry you to work. And because you must
pay the same every evening to wait in the cold
to be jerked and stopped and jerked and stopped
all the way back to the house. Fifty cents a day
taken out of the dollars squeezed from the body's labor
so at the end of the day, the body can be hauled to where it stays
     overnight
can enter the black bedrooms, be lit by a candle
and eat bread and cold milk.

Lastly the poem wants Gordon Shrum to die
because at a meeting he reached over to my friend Mark Warrior
and smacked him in the mouth.
He was charged and duly acquitted
because Mark was shouting out at the time how the French
were finally getting off their knees
and striking back at the bullies that push them, at the men like
     Shrum
—whom Mark didn't name.

But whom I name, with his bureaucrats and service division
his credit office and transportation system. Him, and
every other animal who is gnawing away at our lives.
May before they die
they know what it is like to be cold, may the cold eat into them
may they live so they cough all night and can't sleep
and have to get up the next morning for work just the same.
May the joints of their bodies swell with their labor
and their backs ache. And before they die
may they know deeply, to the inside of their stomachs
the meaning of a single word:
unemployment. May they understand it

as the nourishment a man gets by scraping the calendar over a
   pan for a meal.
May they have a future with nothing in it
but unemployment; may they end on welfare.

May they have to travel by bus
to get their welfare. May they wake in the night and realize
that for the rest of their lives they will never eat together
all the things they love: steak and wine and hot corn.
They will never have these together again until they die.
May they die on welfare.
And may the Lord God *Jesus* have mercy on their souls.

■   THE THREAD

A loose thread at my shirt cuff.
I pull
and it unwinds around my sleeve.
As I tug, I glance ahead
to guess how far it will unravel.
In the distance, I observe the thread leading
to the machine of a woman in Seoul
who assembled my garment. I hear her voice
above the noise of the factory:
Most people in this district
act as if it is our destiny to be poor.
But is that right? We work from seven in the morning
until eleven-thirty in the evening. Our skin turns color
because of less chance to be outside.
Also my hands have many wounds
from the sewing. And sometimes I can't open my eyes
in strong sunlight. I don't know the name
of that disease.

From the bobbin she touches
the thread unrolls eastward
to the cotton plants of a man in Texas.
If I kneel where his tractor pulls a plow
through the rich soil
I can see where the thread starts.

A foot or so below the surface
the thread joins the top of a ball of twine
enormous as the planet. If I place my fingers and palm
on this tightly-wound sphere
I can feel its vibrating hum.

I reach the same destination
when my thick fingers take hold of some matter
caught between my teeth. I yank
and what pulls free
is the beginning of a great looping wire
generated by supermarket clerks, long-haul drivers,
stoop harvesters, seed merchants
that also extends back to the earth.

This is why I am certain
what passes through our lives
inextricably links us with each other.
And that nothing we encounter is ours alone.
There is no way to sever,
to possess a portion of twine.
Men and women can use a length of cable
for a whip or noose. They can pollute a section
with poison or slime. Yet these debased bits of string
do not belong to them completely
despite their bragging.

Moments after each of us is born
the umbilical cord is cut.
But other fibres that tie us to our parents
commence at once to stretch
into bands that feed us and join us to the rest of the room
and beyond. We remain enmeshed our entire lives,
pulling the net this direction and that
as we travel and age, the web that holds us
flexible enough to let some of us journey to the moon.
Yet the anchor
of each of the million cords that wrap me,
that connect me to justice and injustice,
remains that closely-wound, pulsing ball
of global string.

Even these words
were handed to me
containing the grammars and syntaxes
others built and tore down
and constructed again, new verbs
forming, and nouns
appearing in my mouth or from under my pen:
airborne seeds from elsewhere
that find root in my days
—some destructive, some helpful,
each word trailing a resilient tendril,
another thread
that weaves me and all I do
into the warp of our world.

■ LOCAL TRAFFIC

HIGHWAY 2 NORTH OF EDMONTON, ALBERTA

The glow of the city slips behind
as the car speeds into the blackness.
My high beams uncover a road
constructed during the day
across a landscape now invisible.
Out here, in the night
that is half our world,
are also trees, barns, cultivated fields.
But in light's absence
these exist unseen.

                    Most of the universe
consists of darkness. The stars
and their planets huddled as near them as possible
are only an insignificant imperfection
in cold space. In this age, we bring our lamps
into the dark beyond the towns
to reveal what waits there
unaffected by our feeble spark:

       Jupiter floating among its moons,
       three hundred times more massive than the Earth,
       its outer shell immense bands of
       turbulent, swirling cloud

                    or the ruined ocean liner
       that fell for hours
       into the abyss, to rest on the sea floor
       eerily upright, surrounded by a spray
       of human objects—
       cutlery, shoes, ropes, eyeglasses, stoves

as in the houses
along this highway
hidden from me, or located
by a single light
gleaming on the dark hills.

■ RESTING BY A CREEK AT THE CAPE SCOTT TRAILHEAD

Like the world, in this world
are water people and pebble people.
The water people move quickly,
musically. They are confident
their actions finally will wear down rock.
The pebbles do not speak
except if stepped on
or rolled. But they understand
the virtues of stability.
Their steadiness
lets them observe the water people are gone downstream
before they can know the effect they had in this place.

Yet a droplet gleams on a stone.
Shining at the bottom of the creek is gravel.

And this stream
has turned part of a mountain to sand.
While below here, on the Pacific, silt
from these pebbles
is filling up San Josef Bay.

■ WATSONVILLE

As I cross south Santa Cruz county
near the Monterey line
the fields flashing past stretch
far as the dim hills
Rows of the jagged leafy artichoke
or avocado
the air thick with
a salty vegetable odor

                    And the moon
burning over Monterey Bay

Everything visible in this place
has been worked
I talked tonight to a young man

whose eight hours are loading pallets
of cabbages into trailer-trucks with a forklift
for the minimum wage
His partner loads the lettuce
At least the forklifts are
electric, he says, propane exhaust
in the box of a trailer is bad

And a young woman
who adjusts accounts
at a local department store
The codes to key into her machine
are familiar to her
as her name, the anxious customers on the phone
often stupid or hostile

But from the lives and the soil here
half a continent eats
Though the sea looks barren, it also is turned
by the sharp keels
of the fishboats, harvesters on the moonlit fields
gather what has grown below the surface

    And even the moon
    at this date has footsteps and tire tracks
    in its dust
    The sailors who completed their tasks aloft
    picked up their pay at the end of the voyage
    like any other deckhand
    or mate

And I
have driven twelve hundred miles to these counties
that feed my city, too
in a different country
This land and people teach me
what to curse
to praise
as I speed through the American years
under the working moon

■ CANADIAN CULTURE: ANOTHER RIEL POEM

And when they went to honor Louis Riel
they first made him larger than life,
then stripped him, lashed his wrists
behind his back, and bent him forward
as if pleading or in pain
and constructed a statue of him in this guise
behind the parliament buildings at Winnipeg.
To further mark the shame
of his failure to defeat the government of Canada
they erected two high cement semicircles
to conceal the representation of him.
Around the base of these
they placed in English and French
Riel's quote: ''I consider myself to be
the founder of Manitoba.''
They carefully didn't say he *was*
the founder, just that he believed himself such,
thus leaving the issue open-ended,
dependent on your point of view
—in other words, unresolved, confused
or what they insist is
Canadian.

But when I strolled along the path
beside the Assiniboine in 1987
to see the statue for myself
I found some person, screened by the cement walls
that bracket Riel,
had taken a hammer
and smashed off his genitals
and gouged a hole in one bent knee.
There was nothing indecisive
about this act, this mutilation
conducted in secret
by the powerless.
And where the hammer landed
a chickenwire frame for the statue was evident.
This image of failed revolt
is not even marble

but an imitation: some other hard substance
formed over a hollow core.

When I asked various citizens of Winnipeg
about the damage
they said it had occurred months previously.
The authorities, apparently, were content to display Riel
in this condition: bound helpless,
struck at and spat upon
by those he meant to aid
—an image they prefer
for rebels, for a politics outside parliaments,
an authorized location for our blows to fall
safely out of sight
a block or so from the traffic
over the Osborne Street bridge.

■   AT THE KOOTENAY GATES

Flow on, green waves of mountains
lifting my car on your surges,
carrying me along the narrow threads of asphalt
toward your heart. Spruce and pine
cover your high August slopes, cedar and
fir lower down, then the first square farmhouse
balanced on a ledge, beside hay
and the green corn
of the valley floor; sawmills
and heavy truckloads of cut lumber
shake the valleys deeper, as hawks and
an osprey
ride up the thermals, to turn against the bright clouds
and gaze back at

winter:

        the forests still, only the roads
and smoke from the settlements moving
at the base of the huge white waves.

■ RV'S

In early spring
they are let out of the small barns
or yards behind houses
where they have been tethered all winter.

They feel a pull toward
the open or forested country
beyond cities or towns. So they appear on the highways
singly, then in bigger numbers
until by June they have formed their summer family groupings
and herds. They sway in long files
up the mountain roads
and plod through the settled valley bottoms.
Three species are readily identifiable:
self-propelled, towed
and loaded-onto-pickups. Most columns, however,
consist of a mix. But every type
is an obstacle
to the car and tractor-trailer drivers
in line behind them
who curse these creatures' apparent ignorance
of the hour and the dollar.

Yet the vast distances of our continent
cry for something this large
and ponderous. The buffalo guns' final shots
were still ringing, the last of the great shaggy beasts
were just penned in corrals and parks
when the first motorized replacement
coughed, shook itself alive
and stumbled into the fields.
The persistence here of the bulky,
the slow
instructs us
these lands are not to be swiftly passed through
and that where we are heading
is not
where we are.

■ KOOTENAY GREEN (12% ALCOHOL BY VOLUME)

Horsetail and sword
ferns, from the roadside.
In the silence, the spicy odor
of the woods—cedar and larch,
pine and fir. From the pastures
cattle and the lithe deer,
bear in the ditches
or skirting chicken coops,
Russian vegetable gardens or
discovered in someone's fruit tree.
Along the highways
the settlements contribute
heavy equipment mechanics and
part-time prospectors,
spinners and dyers, mill workers
as, above,
huge sheets of spruce climb
toward the sky: giant steps
of bluffs and empty cliffs, then
wooded benches lifting
to the snowy meadows and
peaks
closest to Heaven.
While down through everything
flow the waters—creeks and
streams
noisy, yeasty,
then wide-running
as the local wine
aging in cold cellars or storerooms
to be brought out and
poured
in the clear cup
of each
hour.

■ *SEA-CAT*

In the stream of waves
flowing up the inlet, the *Sea-Cat*
nods at the anchored dock,
her lines secure. From shore
her thirty-eight feet look trim as ever
this spring, but anybody close
could see paint missing
from her wooden cabin, cracks
below her decks and around a porthole.

She is owned by a family
who nosed her into the Strait for years
toward forested coves and unfamiliar harbors
all along the raincoast.
In today's bright weather, she quivers
as one of the grown sons
steps aboard to check her bilge.
The tarp covering her stern is pulled back,
the cabin door unlocked
but inside
are half-finished repairs
and lumber, unstowed
cutlery and plates, torn charts, an old sweater
jammed onto a shelf.
Her hull is sound, the son says. But
the battery wires to her diesel
have corroded, glow-plugs
won't heat enough to light,
suddenly smoke
rises from behind a bulkhead. The key is withdrawn;
another thing to fix. The cabin door is shut,
tarp secured.

       And she floats alone,
the light from the sun
down the channel
pouring into her windows
and old wood
sailing into a different season.

■ VANCOUVER WINTER

Like cats at a window
the houses along the wet street
look out at the downpour.

In the window of a house
a cat. In the cat's eye

drenched asphalt, the line of houses,
smoke from the chimneys streaming toward the ground
through the sodden air.

■ WAITING FOR MAIL

All morning I listen for mail.
Whatever the letter carrier totes up the stairs
will be a break from the papers on my desk.
Most often, if anything good
is to happen today
it will be pushed through my door slot.

But when the person with the mail
enters my neighborhood
every dog for blocks
starts to bark and howl.

What is it dogs understand about mail
that I don't?

■ INITIAL REPORT
after Yehuda Amichai

I would have preferred
to employ an investigator. But I lacked the means
and had to go myself. I could view my thirties
from my twenties; it was the forties I was doubtful about.

This far, I can report
the terrain of my fourth decade

looks rather familiar.
The inhabitants seem content, if often complacent.
They vary greatly in appearance, however,
so I'm not always sure whether I'm talking to residents
or tourists from either of the adjoining states.

And some of my assessment has to be
subjective. I raced most of the distance here as usual
but as I entered the region
I was overcome by a sense of
speeding toward a dark unpleasantness.
I'm aware this observation is vague
with little value as intelligence.
Yet though I feel no loss of energy or skill
and my limbs and breath remain as sound as ever
I don't think I should examine this territory
at my accustomed pace.
I realize you would like
a complete account as rapidly as possible.
But my experience elsewhere convinces me
I can't accurately understand a locale or social structure
unless I work in it, confront it,
cause it to act under stress
—which is hard to do
while darting through it.

Expect more dispatches soon.
But if you want a quick summary
then on to my fifties
you'll have to send somebody else.
If I find the place interesting, I plan to settle
for a bit. Or this might even be where
I'll end up.

■   HATING JEWS

How much work
it must be to despise the Jews.
Fourteen million people, or more:
a majority of whom you've never met

but every one
has to be hated. Anti-Semites surely deserve some credit
for undertaking this collosal task.

And speaking of Semites, what about women and men
who hate Arabs? There are more Arabs
than Jews: some who dwell in the desert
and can't read or write,
some who ride around in air-conditioned limousines
rich as Jews are supposed to be.
What an effort is required
to detest so many social groups:
urban, nomads, electronic
specialists, nurses, irrigation technicians.

Meantime, certain individuals
loathe Orientals. I think these haters
should receive an international prize
for their willingness to abhor such a high percentage
of their own species. But others
hate homosexuals
or lesbians, or all men
or women—the latter two projects
being probably the largest ever initiated
in human history.

Yet having an aversion
only to Jews
is such a mammoth endeavor
no wonder those who tackle it
look drained: faces twisted, body slumped.
A few pros after years of training
carry it off more comfortably.
But ordinary women and men who sign up for this activity
seem to my eyes heavily burdened.

And me? I am repulsed
by those human beings who do me harm.
I'm not as ambitious as
the big-league despisers, though.

I attempt to focus my disgust
on specific individuals
causing pain to myself or my friends.
It's true I've learned to dislike
some general classifications of people
—for example, landlords and employers.
But rather than loathe each one of them
I try to remember the source of their odiousness
is the structure that gives them
their power over me
and aim my rage at that.

So I'm not against hate. I consider some of it
excellent for the circulation: enough injustice
remains on this planet
to justify hate being with us a while yet.
My intent is
to see it directed
where it will do the most good.

■ WEAK THINGS

Weak things have power.
The strong of this world
don't want you to notice, but consider plants:
what could be more passive?
We walk on the grass, for example,
dogs do worse to it.
Yet a tiny portion of a ground-up plant
can poison you
or cure you of sickness
or get you high. Animals
receive most of the attention
as they race around, barking and
gnashing their teeth.
But the oxygen animals require to live
is given off by plants as waste.
The plants don't even have a use
for the noisy, self-important creatures

except in a few cases as an alternate strategy
for spreading seeds.

                    Or consider poems.
"No one reads poetry; it's a dying art."
Yet people of all ages
go on silently writing poems
which means they must fulfill some urge.
"Poets are their own greatest enemies.
What they write, you can't understand."
True at times, but words you *can* comprehend
mostly intend to sell you an idea or object
that needs to be carefully examined
to see if, despite its glossy appearance,
it is hurtful to you—
examined closely
as a difficult poem.
"Well, nobody *buys* poetry." Okay,
yet as people continue to appreciate poems
something is cherished on this planet
that can't be converted to a cash equivalent.
What else do we value that doesn't involve money?
Would you attend a church so poor
it meets in an open field? Do you possess a single item,
besides poems, that no one was *paid* to produce?

Jesus said the meek would inherit. Not that strength
is bad, but often those who have it forget
the flesh of even the strongest
is composed mainly of water.
Only the truly weak are free of
the temptation to dominate, to harm.
That is why democracy is about weakness,
why it is to the weak we turn for help
when we are beaten, condemned.
This is why poems continue
like the air.

■ PICNIC IN A RUNAWAY LANE

Those who arranged to lead us
left us at this spot.
We brought blankets, hibachis,
portable lawn chairs
and hampers filled with food and
drinks. All day on this steep lane
that rises from the highway
we've eaten and rested, talked,
played games with the kids
or watched them race along the ruts
farther up the hillside.

Nearly always present
is the roar of traffic.
The mountain road curves here
and as a precaution if truck brakes fail
or a driver ends in the wrong gear
and the braking system can't hold the trailer weight
this slope was prepared to allow gravity
to save the vehicle and its contents.

Between us and the country around
is a wire fence and ''No Trespassing'' signs.
Our leaders have assured us
statistically at this site there is little chance
of a mishap. And the lane provides a clear area
for personal enjoyment
as well as a unique view down the grade.

Our leaders predicted correctly
a few complainers would object to this location.
And that some of the descending truckers
would be hostile,
releasing a blast
from their airhorn at us
and gesturing wildly as they pass.
But other drivers we consider friendlies
give a cheerful wave and toot of the horn
while they rumble by.

In the dusk, however, it has become difficult to tell
a driver's intention.
The deep sound of the horn
from approaching trucks
is hard to interpret.
Once, the rear tires on a trailer
of a truck travelling too fast
touched the shoulder just up the road.
We'd seen that happen by day:
the dust lifting and hanging
as the rig disappeared down the curve.
But at night, the clatter of this one
has started the children crying
and resulted in a stir among the adults.

Many people have packed
and stand at the edge of the asphalt
as if waiting to leave.
Above the straining engines
they speak to their neighbors
of the fine time they had today.
Now they want to go elsewhere.
But they are vague about how this can occur.
They stare at oncoming headlights
as though they believe one pair will
by previous agreement
stop for them.

While night has deepened, the number of trucks
has increased. The lights streaming toward us
now form an unbroken line
and the noise as they fight to complete the turn
is more and more unpleasant.
An argument has begun
about whether we should light fires
against the cool night air
and to demonstrate we are here.
Or if this would distract or
enrage the truckers
and so place us
in danger.

■ THE SHADOWS OF THE AFTERNOON

We stopped at midday
where the trail
wound down through the tangled
woods to skirt a lake for more than a kilometre.
At a clearing beside the path
we leaned our packs against stumps
or the trunk of a large windfall and
wriggled free of the straps.
Sweat was suddenly chill on my back
through my soaked shirt.
But my body and legs felt as light as
if gravity had been temporarily suspended.

I could see, across the lake's still surface
the wake of a loon
propelling itself toward the forest on the other shore.
Like my companions, though,
I bent to dig out my compact stove
and pot, matches, soup mix.
At the boggy edge of the lake, I scooped water
and returned to set it to boil.

There was not much noise
for so many people. We had begun
full of chatter, but the steady efforts of the morning
had quieted us, as we climbed and
descended while the trail unrolled
between firs and cedars under a distant roof of leaves
or crossed into a bright glade
with salmonberry bushes taller than ourselves
on the slope alongside.

The sounds in this clearing
were just a few low voices, as each person or group
crouched over plates and bowls
by the hissing stoves.
And birds: robin and crow and jay.
Someone had lit a small fire.

Next to each of us
was an unbuckled pack;
the opened pouches offered a glimpse
of our personal needs: clothes, binoculars,
food, a guitar. And tucked in among them
were tools for the work
we were journeying to accomplish:
gasoline, chainsaw engine,
a rifle, nails, sewing gear,
hoes. Only the youngest children
walked free.

                       While we ate, the place
started to seem familiar.
Various patches were now
specific people's territory; this was
the common route to water.
But as we readied ourselves to leave
—compressing the objects we had dispersed
into tighter form once more—
the clearing again was
a space in the undergrowth
with some fallen logs and
now-trampled bushes and grass:
what we left
as we hoisted our packs
and stood on the trail to resume our passage
strung out single file
in the midst of a wood.

And this is how I will travel
the remainder of this day.
Part of a relentless column
I step occasionally
by those taking a break
or pause to rest for a minute myself.
Committed with others to an uncertain venture
and with the weight of all I support
tugging at my back,

I proceed
through the shadows
of the afternoon.

■ THE VALLEY

> ''Look for me here...''
> —*I Will Come Back*, Neruda

If I am no longer found
bending above a concrete slab
to file a metal sheet's rough edge,
or standing in the hum of fluorescent lights
in front of a chalkboard
talking, or seated at my desk at home
scratching at my papers with a pen

I will be on an interstate
in Southern Oregon
where twin lines of asphalt
crest atop a rise
and descend into a valley
ringed by forested hills. Here
I am always the traveller
speeding among the B-trains
—tractors that pull two semi-trailers—
and the A-trains—a tractor, one semi-
and one true trailer: the eight axles
carrying the weight of the load
or deadheading empty
back to Ashland or Red Bluff.

Instead of words
in my ears will be the sounds of the wind
against my car
and of the tires and motors of vehicles that pass me
or that I overtake.
This morning
the cleared fields and woods around me are green

and the air still moist
after the night's rain.

My hands grip the wheel.
And if I glance down to ensure
the pointers of the dashboard gauges
are within normal limits
I notice the face of the clock
is blank
like an indicator that displays a lighted symbol
should oil pressure become low
but is invisible when all is well

—as now, the engine running without a flaw
as I head forever
into this valley

completely happy.

ENIGMAS

■ AFTER FAILURE

After failure, I enter into
a zone or bubble of silence.
I continue to travel, but the rage and echo of voices
including my own
sound fainter and fainter astern. I coast
within a smoothness wrapped in quiet—
not large, but protective
and beautiful: a pod lined with mother of pearl
soft to the touch, thick, insulating.
Nothing is asked of me, in this fragile
but resilient space
that carries me forward.

And when this zone docks
at the edge of another area
for me to disembark
the mating will be evident
only by the slightest click
and an almost imperceptible rocking motion,
quickly stilled.

■ THE RUNNERS

As I strolled the seawall
in the rain, clouds low
above the inlet,
three men jogged past me with such an effortless stride
I suddenly took up their pace
behind them. I don't think they
were a lot younger than me
or older, but they stepped easily
through the downpour,
large-bodied, talking in a friendly manner
to each other. They didn't seem to mind
me joining them, called back
greetings and a few questions
about the weather

as we pounded along, skirting puddles
and dodging umbrellaed walkers
on the path. I knew I was in no shape
for this, but remembered people's opinions
that mine are runner's legs, and continued
yet saved my breath rather than
say much to the others.
I had no idea
where we were running to,
they with their wide shoulders
and confident stride
but I felt no matter what obstacles
or quest we faced
if anyone could win
it was men like these.
Or maybe we were running for nothing,
splashing through the afternoon rain
only to run. And soon I
was too busy keeping my body with them
to care about where we were going.

■ BIRDS, IN THE LAST OF THE DARK

Birds, in the last of the dark
or the orange dawn, start to sing
—often waking me.
Their insistent calls
each morning
are audible for blocks
from May
until I am aware of a silence
deep in the autumn.
If I am up
walking away through the silvered streets,
empty and perfect as a drawing's,
I hear different birds
also singing.

As their notes
around my tent on a beach

a hundred miles northwest of here
pull me from dreams
of the forest.

This singing
extends like a grid
every place I am
and am not: the other life
revealed in this life,
an alternate
world
not calling to rouse us
but calling

at the edge of the light

■ THERE IS A LOVE WITH A WOUND

There is a love with a wound
A wound I put there

Like a blow
That caves in the body

Or a boulder
Half-buried in a lawn

Even if I treat that wound
It won't disappear completely

When the stone is taken away
The raw earth will be visible

And after the grass spreads
Across the place torn open

A depression will remain

For now, though, I love
Around a wound

A wound I put there

■ THE BIRDS CIRCLING THE HIGH MOUNTAINS

The birds circling
The high mountains where we met
Are dead now

Their children call to each other
Under the rainy skies

Four years have almost passed
Someone who entered college that year
Is entirely changed, a baby

Who was just born
Now runs to its mother to
Ask for something

Birds here
Drop and lift on the waves
And the rain falls into the sea

■ THE POET MILTON ACORN CROSSES INTO THE REPUBLIC OF HEAVEN

Somewhere west of his death, he stood
before a tall cottonwood or alder.
As on an autumn afternoon, the leaves
had turned to luminous yellows, shaking
in a wind, the motions of blades and stems
at times swaying to a unified falling and lifting
then back into hundreds of different flurries.

The walls of a bluff or canyon
rose behind the tree. And he saw
high in the branches
or the air, an energy
made visible, a cloud
drifting toward him.
When it touched ground, it took the form

almost of a person
blurred by a light emanating from itself
although appearing to be dressed in a white gown
with waist-length wings.

He was determined not to be awed
by anything metaphysical.
His hand reached for the shirt pocket
where he usually kept his cigars. Nothing.
''You're an angel?'' he asked, gruffly as he could.
Despite himself, his voice sounded nervous
to his ears. *No.* The sweet accent
was neither male nor female.
This is a shape meant to be familiar to your species.

His hand shook slightly
as he patted his other shirt pocket.
Empty. He cleared his throat.
''As a dialectical materialist,'' he said,
''I have to tell you
your wings are too short.
I read once for a human-size body to stay airborne
its wings would need to be pretty damn large.''
The figure in front of him shimmered.
While he strained to focus, the figure's wings
extended to reach the dusty soil.

''Much better,'' he said, attempting to keep the initiative.
''You wouldn't have a cigar on you?''
No response. He shrugged.
''Well, if you aren't an angel, are you a saint?
St. Peter, perhaps? Ready to judge if I'm worthy to pass
the Pearly Gates?'' He jabbed out a finger.
''I never believed in
any afterlife. I used to say I wouldn't want to spend eternity
with any of the pious frauds and criminals
they're always telling us on Earth
get to go to Paradise.''

There is only one life, the figure said.

''Then how is it I'm speaking with you?''
he replied. A cold gust shook the leaves.
The poet shivered.

Do you feel you merit an everlasting existence?
The figure's voice was curious.

''If I had to, I could testify to God himself
—or herself, come to think of it—
I was honest,
true to my class, my country, my art.
I was a good carpenter,
a builder first with wood, then words.
I spoke out for what I believe.
I shouted, 'Love!' ''

Some days your mind fogged,
the figure said gently.
It wasn't your fault. But evil and good,
master and victim
became confused for you toward the end. You roared
at the helpless as well as the guilty.

Then he remembered
events he could not know before
and he felt ashamed.
After some moments, he muttered:
''I worked with what I had, didn't I?''

It's unimportant now, the figure said.
Those things occurred in history. Here
you are out of time.
Soon you will abandon
the personality you grew, forever.

A gust sent some of the intense yellow leaves
spiralling from the branches.

''Then why this talk?'' he asked, bitterly.
''I thought when I died I would just disappear.

This is cruel: to bring me back
for a stupid chat. To have to die again.
I was disappointed by much when I was alive.
I never dreamed I would be disappointed by death.''

It's cruel to be born, the figure said.

''Don't give me crap!'' he replied.
Then, calmer,
''If it's going to end for me now,
actions speak louder than words.
Let me see God.''

What? The figure sounded astonished.

''Yeah. If there really is one.
I want to make sense
of what happened, of meeting you.
That would make more of this fit together.''

If you want to see God, you can,
the figure said.
And where the figure had been
a shape contracted
and swirled away, as if smoke,

so the poet saw the great tree
with the wind
like all the winds of the world
stirring the golden leaves.
Then stillness in the branches.
Then a wind again.

That is God, the voice of the figure said
from the air.

And as he watched the tree breathe,
he entered
the republic of the dark.

■ IN A SMALL HOUSE ON THE OUTSKIRTS OF HEAVEN
after Zbigniew Herbert

In a small house on the outskirts of Heaven
I met the poet. He was on crutches,
one leg in a cast, angry as ever.
''I thought we were raised up in the body
whole and perfect,'' I said to soothe him.
What a joke, he agreed, bitterly. *But if you head downtown*
you can find all that fairy-tale nonsense:
streets of gold and people with perfect complexions
and gorgeous robes, lazing around as if their sole concern
is to improve their technique on the harp.
That's not for the majority, though.
I broke this leg when I slipped on a ladder
at the jobsite. They're expanding the suburbs like crazy.
Most of the new housing is for people like us;
it's junk I'm ashamed to help build.

This bungalow was unfinished outside
with white siding covering the bottom half of the walls
and the rest still insulation paper. Steep stairs
led from the front walk to the main floor.
The yard was mounds of dirt
and piles of scrap lumber. A battered tricycle
was tipped over near a heap of sand
on which was a toy bulldozer minus one tread
and a plastic boat.

                    ''Somebody else lives here?''
I asked. *I rent the upstairs,* the poet said.
A single mother is in the basement.
It's a horrible way to have to raise a kid.
''You pay rent?'' I said. ''You have to earn a living?
This isn't how I imagined Heaven to be.''
You thought the rich would suffer for their crimes?
he blustered. *The poor would be rewarded?*
Not in this universe. The Old Authoritarian
likes everything as it is. Life here is exactly as fair

as where we came from. We had it correct when we were alive:
make things more just on Earth
and you improve Heaven, too.

"You mean there's no hope?"
This ain't Hell, he said sharply. *Of course there's hope.*
He poled himself across the room
and gently lifted a cat off some papers on a chair.
A few of us have begun to hold meetings.
Look. Started our own paper.
We're exposing conditions in the building trades.
Worse than any non-union job you ever worked.
Nobody has to put up with this,
not once they understand they're entitled to better.
Two bits.

"Two bits?" I said.
Yeah, he said, thrusting the paper toward me.
I have to ask you to pay for it,
otherwise we won't be able to keep publishing.
I'm laid off with the leg
and Compo in this place is as big a laugh as on Earth.
"I don't have any money," I said.
"I've only been here a short while."
Then take it. He passed me the sheets of newsprint
and swiveled to rummage among the other papers on the chair.
Got some back issues, too.
Pay me when you can. He straightened
and turned to face me, both hands full.
We're having a picket tomorrow. Our first action
as a group, where one of our members works.
We have to be at the factory by six-thirty a.m.
He held out a leaflet.
See you there?

◼ A YELLOW COTTAGE

■ A YELLOW COTTAGE

1

Transparent waves
Of the lake
Slap
Onto stones and sand
Behind which steps of planks and earth
Lead up a steep bank

To a yellow cottage
One of many dwellings
That line this
Summer bay
From here
The miles of water
Reach Long Duck Island
Then wooded shores
Without houses, except
The tiny dock
Of a monastery
Then
Other islands

To the north end, where a creek
Winds back from a cove
Through marshes
And stands of maple and birch to
The first in a chain
Of empty lakes
The dirt roads
Swinging south once more
Or stopping
As the water retraces a path
Among forest and
Distant mountains
To the edge of
The icy sea

2

A flat stone
Taken up from the beach

Held
Like this

And spun
Toward the sun-sparkling

Lake

An adult's hand
Propelling the stone

So it bounces
Once, twice, more

On the shimmering
Water

While a child's fingers
Scratch amid pebbles

Grasp another stone
Fling it

Down into clear waves

No, this way
Again the adult hand

Skips a stone
Circle to circle

That hand then shows hands
How to choose

How to hold
To throw

51

And the child's toss this
Time

       Strikes
And lifts

       Soars
And lands

       Soars
The stone suspended

The child's fingers

Lengthening, becoming graceful

In the bright air

3

Up at the cottage
Sounds of the birds, faint boat engines
The voices of children
From a neighbor's
Or along the lane

Trees
Around the house
Rustle

Their foliage
A shifting pattern
Of shadow
On a yellow wall

On the wood porch floor

A white wall
Indoors, beside a window

4

Under this August sun
A woman
Is dying

Neither very young nor old, she waits
Below the noisy leaves
Watching her children play

Where she played
Much has changed, nothing
Has changed

Her parents
Still spend the hot days
Swimming, canoeing

With children, now
Grandchildren

Across the lane
In Yelle's field
Grasshoppers

Leap through the tall hay

Grasshoppers to be caught
Cupped
In an adult's hand, a child's

Hand
And let free

5

One morning
She picks up a pail
For berries
And goes out the cottage door

She hugs each
Of her two young daughters, they
Demand to go with her
As before, but she

With her sad
Beautiful face
Sighs and

Kisses them. She embraces
Her husband
Her parents
Sisters, brother, friends

And starts to
Walk through the fields
Toward the hill

Where berries
Grow: straw-
Berries on the upland meadows
Raspberries higher in the tangled brush

As she has loved to
Girl and woman
She wants to gather, to eat while picking
And bring home

She climbs
And sees beyond a wood on the near shore
The blue cloud of the lake
And the far Laurentians
At last, in a favorite spot
She reaches to touch
The red fruit amid
The green thorns
Placing one berry
In her mouth to
Savor
The sudden pure

Delight, she sets to work
To provide
This joy again
For the others down the hill
For all her world

Until her fingers
Discover on a stem
A pulpy
Discolored hybrid
She holds for a moment
A dark
Lump
She brings to her lips

6

Lake water
Cools the body when immersed
In the heat of day
Or warms it
After dark

In a boat's shadow
Reeds and mud are visible
On the bottom

Minnows school
Above stones or
Furrows of sand

7

Lake air
Brings light
To the veins of the leaves
To nourish
And consume

Over this rocky shore

Where a spirit
Has left the earth

And remains

DEFECTIVE PARTS OF SPEECH

■ DEFECTIVE PARTS OF SPEECH: TOUCHING THE INNER LIFE

In severe hypothermia, perhaps caused
by prolonged immersion in
a teacher's or leader's voice,
the extremities of the body should be ignored
though they can be as blue and chilled
as newsmagazines or television. Instead
the patient has to be warmed from
the inside: a hot fluid, like coffee or soup,
is needed to raise the temperature
of the inner core—brain, lungs, digestive organs.
Help applied first to the visible symptoms
will drive cold blood
inward, further lowering
the vital central temperature.

In worse cases, a warm saline solution
is introduced to the stomach,
then flushed out and the procedure repeated.
Oxygen passed through a heat source
can be given, and an IV started
to assist in restoring the circulatory system.

But in critical situations
the person must be cut open
and the heart warmed directly.

■ DEFECTIVE PARTS OF SPEECH: OFFICIAL ERRATA

Where it says *welfare* read *suffering*
''The seasonally-adjusted rate of suffering
fell one per cent last month.''
Where it says *defense* read *suffering*
''The Department of Suffering confirmed Friday
the shipment of $1 billion in new tanks and helicopters
to friendly governments in Latin America.''

Where it says *productivity* read *suffering*
''Canadian industry must increase the suffering of its employees
at least 12 per cent this year.''
Where it says *co-operation* read *suffering*
''The administration requires the suffering of every citizen
to see us through these difficult times.''

Where it says *efficiency* read *suffering*
Where it says *management* read *suffering*
Where it says *suffering* read *defeat*

■ DEFECTIVE PARTS OF SPEECH:
   HIERARCHY

A trout propels itself through water
with a lamprey dangling from its side.
Because the fish does not remember, its lamprey
seems natural as its tail.
The fish long ago learned to correct
for the extra shape and weight
as it swims.

If you watch the fish's eyes
there is no sign it is aware
it is being eaten alive.
The fish part of this dual organism
continues trying to survive and prosper
as a fish. If it sees
a being identical with itself
but without the parasite embedded in its flesh,
draining it,
that too seems ordained:
some of us have this appendage,
others don't
If it notices a fish
with four or five lampreys
suspended, the rasps of their teeth
sunk into its belly
and face

so that fish has become immobile,
listlessly gulping water,
ready to die,
the thought is
*there's a sick
one of us*
If further reasoning were possible
the extra observation might be
*that fish grew more of these limbs
than I did*   But the concept
never flashes into the brain
and the still-useful host
darts away.

■   DEFECTIVE PARTS OF SPEECH:
     ''AN AUXILIARY USED TO EXPRESS NECESSITY,
     DUTY, OBLIGATION, ETC.''

When anyone says
''What you should

do is . . .''

I know my newest problem
is this *SHOULD*

a word
that wants to wrap itself in
authority
as of a royal court

or God

who in fact hasn't been asked
who hasn't spoken

So I urge a rephrasing
''What I suggest
you do . . .''

Now the idea
has to stand alone
without the costume
without the invisible police

said by just an *I*
who faces me
—two human persons

one of whom wishes *should*
obsolete, a relic
preserved only in dictionaries

like kings
priests

and the boss

■   DEFECTIVE PARTS OF SPEECH:
    TRANSLATIONS

I understand how the earth
becomes land.
But not how stone
is also boulder or rock.

Why can heart be soul, at times?
Afternoon fade to evening?

I don't understand.

A simple *is* turns into *hovers*
or worse. Water
becomes drops of water.

History and memory disappear
into a pronoun.

I understand
and don't understand.

Are we moving quickly away?
Blow becomes thump and then sound.

Hunger, homelessness, ignorance:
how can these mean
lack of employment

or the world's confusions
a new puzzle?

I understand
and I don't understand.

■   DEFECTIVE PARTS OF SPEECH:
    MEDIABURN

After hours of watching electrons
form and reform images
or of reading the clipped prose of a daily paper,
the body experiences a chemical change.
The eye or outer skin is not affected
such as follows lengthy exposure to
ultraviolet rays or cold.
Instead, the surface of the
brain
turns raw and inflamed, easily irritated
by new information counter to
what has caused the tissue damage.
This makes treatment difficult.
The patient will resist
those who are attempting to help,
in some cases becoming hysterical
or violent.

            Yet the best salve for this affliction
originates with the patient. She or he must
speak first hand
with people whose activities or attitudes
are being transmitted

or recall events in which he or she participated:
whether accounts of these were accurate.

Once restored to health
a victim seldom is reinfected
—at least to the same extent.
Pessimism about the illness, however,
arises from a lack of
preventative education. This results in
numbers of individuals contracting the ailment
who otherwise might escape
including many who cannnot recognize symptoms
and so are unaware they are diseased.

■ DEFECTIVE PARTS OF SPEECH:
  FOUND

Be cautious about
graphic
language.

This series of texts
is directed at
high school students.
And while they might not blanche
at ''crude'' speech
or descriptions of the
sex act
teachers might.

Our Department of Education
representatives
have allowed us to use
words such as
''bastard''
or ''piss.''

So we are not really
restricted.

■ DEFECTIVE PARTS OF SPEECH:
HAVE YOU REALLY READ ALL THESE?

A wall of books in my house: a giant page of words
made from multicolored letters
formidable

> to some
who have learned instead or
also to read
water, for example
in the bay
with a southeast wind
how the currents and fish respond

or the park warden looking at sign
See? The coyote have been eating the deer.

Ernie Frank stopping where the trail has exposed
soil horizons, showing us
what they reveal

or the mountain guide explaining
how he interprets snow: the amount the crystals tell
by their shape and dampness

You think we didn't have clocks?
the elder asked Sandy Cameron
*The tide was our clock. We understood
the time of day and day of the year
from the tide.*

And the people who decipher accurately
the face of those they love
or hate

My insurance agent who insists
*I know who is most likely to have a car accident
by how they walk into this office.*

Men and women who study
the world
picking up warnings and
diagnoses, remedies
and fables

—all these
and more

■   DEFECTIVE PARTS OF SPEECH: EMPLOYMENT ZEN

Employed, we are taught
the owners are not interested

in our ideas to make a job
easier, more effective

even when the result
would increase profits. After years of

this, if we don't have work
the men and women behind the desks

say: *when the jobs aren't there, you need to
start one. Can't you be*

creative?

■   DEFECTIVE PARTS OF SPEECH:
    SUNDAY

The two came down from the sidewalk
into the green park: the woman first,
the man following. They moved with alcoholic
carefulness: both wearing
jeans, fat layered around the woman's middle,
the thinner man half again as tall as her.

Keep away from me, the woman shouted
over her shoulder, but the tall man plodded after her.
Keep away from me, she repeated as she stopped
just under the trees, and families
and other people sitting on the grass in the shade
looked up to see the man's crushed face
was soaked with tears. *Get away.*

          The woman
started to climb
back toward the traffic once more, but
as she passed the tall man
she pushed at him, so he teetered, off
balance, then she was punching him.
He put out his arms
to steady himself, or grab her
but she staggered sidways
and up the rise
with him a few steps behind.

         As her blows
hit, some women and men
from a group under the trees
stood, and began to walk toward the couple.
At the edge of the pavement, the woman
turned and her fists
were in the tall man's face
repeatedly, so he stumbled,
recoiling, then lurched forward
and the two went down.

         The others
broke into a run, and the first there
pulled the couple apart
and upright. The tall man was crying harder
now, blood from his nose
mixed with the wash from his eyes.
Keep him away from me, the woman demanded
while the others clustered around them.
''You can't follow her, man. She doesn't
want you to.''

            The woman said she
had to meet her son
across the avenue, he would have money
left from what she had given him
for the amusement arcade, she was
out of gas for her car on the other side of
the park, keep that man away or he'll rip
the wires out, if she had gas
she could leave that
man who stood crying hopelessly
with some of the others
talking and talking to him.

                    The woman lunged
to close the gap,
slapping at him. He attempted
to retaliate, but the others
moved them further apart now,
offering opinions and
to do this and advising that.

Her son was
found, broke, and gas money collected
from strangers, while the tall man was held by words
at a drinking fountain near her car.
Bending over the clear water, he tried to clean his face.
But the woman, returning at the head of her parade
of child and some of the others with a gas can,
caught sight of him and veered
toward the drinking fountain
and swung at him. She was
peeled away, and eventually
before the tall man's eyes she got her engine going,
spun the wheels backwards, gravel
flying, raced down the street to a lane,
turned around, and gunned past the man again
and was gone.

            He standing
under the curbside trees
seeing her vanish.

"They choose to fight
in public," my friend said. "This way they know
they won't get a chance to really hurt each other,
like the guys who start a brawl at home
but move down to the bar where they're sure someone
will separate them."

The man stood on the grass
looking away.

I had wanted to call the police.

What I want the police to arrest
is tears.

■   DEFECTIVE PARTS OF SPEECH:
     TWO VISITORS

At noon hour in Toronto
in corridors at the top of an enormous office tower
two visitors are examining an art collection
hung on the walls.

It is a man and his grown son: the man
has been in this headquarters a number of times
hired as a consultant to the company
for certain industrial projects
underway in Canada and South America. Now
he has brought his son to see
with the permission of an executive secretary
the Brazilian primitives
and Canadian moderns
displayed in conference rooms and waiting areas.
The art is owned by the man
who is president of the company
and at the door of his office
the two visitors pause, and peer in:
no one.
Far beneath a row of windows, the city

extends from rail yards
out to a distant haze of tiny structures.
On the opposite wall: framed patterns—
the impressions of Joyce Wieland's lips
as she mouthed the syllables of *O Canada*
onto cloth, and a print of a Charles Pachter streetcar.

But the wall facing the president's desk
is filled by two paintings: to the right
the grey stone inside wall of a prison
with graffiti in French scrawled on it
and in an upper corner a barred window
through which brilliant green leaves
are thrusting in. Under the picture
a card says *FLQ Jail Cell.*
Beside this, equally large
is one of Juan Genoves' black-and-white canvases
from Spain: a man in the centre of the mottled space
cut down by bullets while running
the shock
holding the lifted body above its shadow.

High over Toronto, the two visitors
stare at the paintings. And it seems to me
my father, who has shown me much
has shown me something unexpected here
at the heart of business
of capital—the garrotte in Spain
the wage system there and in Canada and Quebec
and in Brazil, and also there the wire brush
used to comb the flesh
screaming on the torturer's table:

                              perhaps someone
who didn't mean these things, a small boy
crying
with a broken jug at his feet
who will feel relief
when at last he is led away

■ DEFECTIVE PARTS OF SPEECH:
DOING THE WORD'S LAUNDRY

> "Language is speech. You ought to be able to say
> language is speech and then get on with the
> rest of it, but you can't because so few believe
> it."
> —Lew Welch

Language is the air
we take in
we breathe out.
But air, like speech
is shaped to use:
geese honk past, wings working
to push down on air.
Tons of jet plane
above the runway
are also lifted on their wings'
differing pressures of
air. In the shop, compressed
air strikes the blades
whirling in the tools we hold
to build things.

Air is never idle.
Speech, too, cannot be
abstract
but means
to identify
and create what happens
—including the mysteries.
Thus oxygen, carbon
dioxide
and other components
find and are found for
their uses. Only what we don't understand
appears or is decreed
gibberish
but is not

unless someone is
blurring the words
to a purpose.
And it is to some persons'
gain
the world should seem
hazy, dimmed
secretive: dirty air
or glossolalia—religious, artistic
or secular.
And those who would lead us say
I can interpret
for you.

But the words
like air
are historical:
planetary accretion
outgassing
the simplest forms of life
all changed the atmosphere's
composition, that text
altered too by our species—
ozone, radioactivity
pesticides, exhaust

as language
a body's, a mind's
product
is affected by
what we do
and whose talk is official.
Lately, as language
entered an industrial
age, first a vocabulary
was invented
then a transformer—
a device to step-up voltage
that is, power: the word
spoken, typed

enlarged to appear
on posters, enormous
on billboards, and its sound
propelled simultaneously
every place
on the electrons
of the air.

This charged
language
has its intentions:
speech must become
simpler
because when the words are huge
there is room for less of them
when they are loud
there is little point in us
talking, are prevalent
it is hard to pronounce
what is here.
These empowered words
try to crowd out
ordinary speech, to elbow in
on what we say, to jam
our language: *cost benefit*
        your representative
        human resources

Yet the charges
such words carry
result in surface static.
Dust and debris
cling to the exteriors
dulling them
so new words
constantly must be transformed
and brought to us: *job creation*
        terrorist
        privatize

Our language
warps under this use.
Our attempts to utter these words
dirty our mouths.

But we do not stop
speaking

and when the words
are tarnished enough
to be safe to handle

we can try to strip away
their soiled coverings:
the clothes a word must have
to function in the world
but these now stained
dark, a different color

needing to be scrubbed
clean, to be rinsed

restored
back to actual size
letter by letter.

The words
without their clothes
shrink also, unbend
until
ready to be dressed again.

Such cleansing, however
does not prevent
those men and women busy charging up
more of what they
want to put in the air
want us to voice
want to say on our behalf.

At best we
try to protect
ourselves, to make our
speech
work for
us.

■ DEFECTIVE PARTS OF SPEECH: TECHNICAL MANUAL

In the beginning, the heart
pumps good red blood.
But with each misunderstanding
or argument
or wish that is, later, recognized as impossible
a speck of black ash
is deposited.

This happens even when such episodes
end with love.
Yet this is normal. The heart is equipped
with a filter to catch these spots.
To prevent clogging, it is sound policy
to clean this filter periodically. Optimum frequency
depends on the rate
of ash generation. Cleaning is best accomplished
by pleasant surprises: purchase of a new bed
or a vacation trip that is actually enjoyed.
Some residue of ash will
remain, but this does not affect
the heart's ordinary functioning.

Under circumstances, though, where ash is produced
too rapidly for the filter to handle it
the blood in the heart becomes greyish
from the floating and settled dark material.
The body then often routes more blood than usual
to the belly
or the legs and arms, or head
in an attempt to return the blood to a healthy state

by exposure to substances found in these areas.

But this procedure is not effective
except in the short term. Anesthetics are available
to mask any pain or discomfort
resulting from the changes within the heart.
Yet narcotics, too, neither eliminate the cause
of the disorder, nor stop the eventual
spread of contaminated blood throughout the body.

To clear the heart at this point
requires more drastic measures.
People typically put off consenting to them
in the belief a cure is worse than the disease.
And those who do successfully undergo treatment
behave like former smokers:
declaring everyone afflicted
should immediately follow a course of action
they rejected themselves
time after time.

■ LOST AND FOUND

■ THE POET

> Taken from *A Checklist to Aid in the Detection of Learning Disabilities*

Loses his position on worksheet or page in textbook
May speak much but makes little sense
Cannot give clear verbal instructions
Does not understand what he reads
Does not understand what he hears
Cannot handle ''yes-no'' questions

Has great difficulty interpreting proverbs
Has difficulty recalling what he ate for breakfast, etc.
Cannot tell a story from a picture
Cannot recognize visual absurdities

Has difficulty classifying and categorizing objects
Has difficulty retaining such things as
addition and subtraction facts, or multiplication tables
May recognize a word one day and not the next

■ INSIDE INFORMATION:
TELEPHONE DIRECTORY POEMS

> From *Metro Vancouver White Pages*, Vancouver, BC

1. URBAN HOUSING

House of Brides
House of Buckles
House of Cards

House of Charm
House of Concord

House of Granite
House of Headboards
House of Heat

House of Knives

House of Lloyds

House of Maple
House of Oak & Brass

House of Orange Importers
House of Oriental Imports
House of Robert Hairstyling

House of Salad & Sandwich
House of Schnitzel

House of Vacuums

House of a Million Parts

2. A MAN'S WORLD

Mr. Donut
Mr. Lube
Mr. Messinger
Mr. Mattress

Mr. Sparks Auto Electric
Mr. Sport Hotel
Mr. Spud
Mr. Video

Mr. Munchie's
Mr. Fix-it Towing
Mr. Pump Service
Mr. Lambchop Meats

Mr. Boot 'N Shoe
Mr. Big 'N Tall

3. PLANETARY CONSCIOUSNESS SONNET

World of Dinettes
World of Lobsters
World of Plants

World of Ties
World of Magic
Truck World

World of Nails
World of Electric Trains
World of Air Conditioning

World Realty
World Movers
Color Your World Paints

Kids' World
World of Time

4. THE LADIES

Miss Donut
Lady Lunch
Lady Lincoln Limo Ltd.
Lady Eve

Lady Bug Clothes Rack
Lady Fingers Studios
Ms. Tress Hair Designs
Lady Coffee Services

Lady Mae Uniforms
Lady Luck

5. AUTO MOTIVE

S & M Motors
Rear Ends Only
Swedish Service
Climax Motors
Silent Witness Auto Parts

Auto Spa
Auto-Medic Ltd.
Auto Mind Collision Repair

Sunlight Auto Repair
Fogg Motors Ltd.
Meteor Service
Galaxie Collision
Cosmos Autocare
Hubcap Heaven

■ GREED SUITE

"There's one underlying motive in business shared by all—that's greed. There's nothing wrong with that. We support it wherever it happens."
> —Barbara MacDougall, Minister
> of State for Privatization,
> Government of Canada, 1987

GREED SUITE:
IN THE CHAMBERS OF COMMERCE

men and women exist
miles under the ocean. In a fluorescent-lit capsule
they believe to be the significant part
of the world
everything is artificial
or gaudily packaged elsewhere
for use at these depths. Thick wall coverings
hide the steel sides of this container
erected on the sea-bottom.
But despite massive air-conditioning systems
beads of water collect below the ceilings
and run down, leaving stains and streaks.

There are few windows
in these rooms. What the inhabitants wish to view
is not located outside. The images they prize
are created by themselves: objects people need to purchase,
how people should appear
and behave. Each human being in this enclosure
is convinced a mirror shows
an exact replica of those dreams.

Opinion surveys conclude
the men and women here
are content. Medically, however,
they display symptoms of extreme stress.
After years in these chambers
faces become grey and drawn
from the internal pressure necessary to sustain the structure.
And inhabitants reveal an obsessive fear
not for the physical destruction of their environment
but of personal collapse: loss of nerve
or drive or luck—situations
that under the operational procedures in force
mean automatic expulsion to the surface.

Yet at times the ocean floor shifts

causing the metal construction to groan
as it settles again, cracking plasterboard
and sending shards of ceiling tile
falling onto display cases or tables.
Occasionally, too, an outer rivet fails
so a jet of water
pours into a containment area built for this purpose
separated by bulkheads from the central portion of the capsule.
The equipment and techniques for repairing such damage
are well established, though. The event receives
only a few paragraphs
on the reassuring nightly news.

■   GREED SUITE:
    THE EMPTINESS OF BUSINESS

When you sell, contempt
is what you feel
People who won't buy
are stupid, short-sighted
and those who do
are suckers, easily fooled

Yet you
must be a purchaser as well

At the heart of commerce
is deceit
To take your profit
you need materials and labor
at less than their worth
which means you must convince people
to accept less

Then the product has to be sold
for more than your cost
so again men and women must be cheated
told lies, called *unreasonable*
if they balk
Profit is something

generated from nothing—
from getting other human beings
to consent
to the prices you name
Words used to accomplish this
resemble a trait of Japanese:
in that language, a person cannot be addressed
as an equal; everyone is either your superior
or inferior, those you flatter
or patronize

There is no friendship
without obligation: your acts
the acts of others
are deposits or withdrawals
in an investment account, women and men are resources
or worthless

And except as it affects sales
there is no weather

■   GREED SUITE:
    EXCHANGE

Money pulled from a billfold
is a match dragged across ignition paper.
As you pass the dollars over
flames from them leap down
to race along the surface of
the object you are buying.
The seller can only grasp your money
by the ends on fire: as his or her fingers approach
they begin to blister
and smoulder. When the hand returns with your change
the palm is a cup of flames
wavering around the glowing coins.
A scent like
scorched tar
rises.

You gingerly reach for the change.
Your other hand is poised above
the product now yours
blazing on the counter.

■ GREED SUITE:
AUTHORITY

To give someone orders
is to give away a part of yourself.

So when a command is uttered
a tiny piece of organic matter
is torn from the brain or other bodily tissues.

People in authority
adopt various means to deal with these wounds.
Some men and women become brutal, to mask
the irritating, needle-like pain of the cuts.
Others wave reasons for their orders in the air
hoping this fanning motion
will soothe the sharp ache.
The faces of others turn into stone
as they endure the lacerations.
These people believe an endless discomfort
is a virtue, that the strain
of keeping their upper and lower teeth clamped together
is proof of natural superiority.

Whatever techniques those who command adopt
their speech is affected. The hurts
are evident in their voice
despite every attempt at sounding natural.

And to be given an order
is to have a small portion of another's body
pasted onto your flesh.

These orders adhere
but are never seamlessly absorbed.

Men and women who accept too many commands
become grotesquely misshapen
under the accretions of alien tissue.
Their bodies try to adjust to
the growths that swell on their skin
by twitching continually. This motion
plus nodes formed on the vocal cords and tongue
distort their talk. Some of what they speak
presents their ideas in their own idiom.
But some of their conversation repeats
the vocabulary and emphasis of their rulers.

Either situation causes madness.
People in charge often embrace the beliefs
of a flagellant, convinced that
if he or she can only slash open
every inch of their bodies by pronouncing more commands
he or she will be entirely healed.
And of those who defer to authority
a number stagger under the mounting weight
of carved out and bleeding flesh.
These men and women decide this condition is desirable
so they treasure any additions to their burden,
certain each new particle justifies
all he or she has carried for years.

Both types of enthusiast
for obedience
are addicts to pain. Their misery
pollutes the world.

■   GREED SUITE:
    ECONOMIC MEDITATIONS

1

Dollars cannot help you.
You may need them, but dollars

do not need you. They pass

through your hands to others

or, for a time, pile up
with money you already have.

Yet money's allegiance
—besides to its own kind—

is to who sent it into the world
rather than who possesses it.

This is because dollars are the smallest part
of the government that issued them

—a hierarchy not developed
for your benefit. Dollars are

reptiles: devoid of affection for the human race.
Though you bring them into your home

or even worship them
they do not care about your fate.

Perhaps this indifference
is why many people believe

money is the perfect means to assess worth.
But dollars, in spite of their travels,

retain a narrow outlook. They resemble the tourists
who demand identical accommodations and amenities

every place. How could these judge
what lies beyond their experience?

2

Advertising is propaganda for dollars
because advertising assures us everything is for sale.

Yet most of the cosmos has no relation to money
so the values of the dollar

are aberrant. That is why dollars ruin
most interactions between people

and between people and their planet. The dollar,
however, is only a metaphor

—an invention thought up on a Thursday afternoon
that seemed a fine idea.

Except, money behaves
like one of those robots in science fiction

that attempts to seize control
over a space ship's crew

or the entire population of the Earth.
To save humanity, we have to

disconnect the function of judgment
money has been assigned,

become the dollar's natural enemy. We must create
a form of exchange

sympathetic to the concerns of men and women,
an artifact

less hateful and solitary.

■ GREED SUITE:
THE CLIMATE

This region is cold as charity
most of the year. Even members of city council
boosting tourism or lobbying for financial incentives
for businesses to locate in the district
fly elsewhere

to seek warmth.
What heat there is
rises suddenly, like lust:
a hot mountain wind melts the snow
in an afternoon, the gutters
are awash as the drains
back up into the streets.
But the asphalt is sheet ice by nightfall
as a frosty chill floats again
under the stars.

And it is a dry
country, almost a desert. Other people's water
has to be bought: trucked in to the public reservoirs
or conveyed large distances in private pipeline systems
whose profit
is guaranteed by the various levels of government.

A constant wind blows
dry and harsh, except for the rare warm gale.
Visitors find the sound of this wind
strange. Indoors or out, you are aware of
men and women speaking
almost beyond earshot. A listener
will believe she or he distinctly hears a word
surfacing from the conversation
that can be pleading, impassioned, soothing
in turn. Nobody
can identify the cause of this phenomenon.
Some geologists speculate
rock formations in an area to the north
once forested, but clear-cut half a century ago,
may induce eddies in the prevailing flow of air
generating an audible frequency.
But this is not proven.

The continual murmur
produces an uneasiness among the residents.
People spend a great deal of money
to insulate their homes from the noise

or to purchase expensive stereo components
or special fans so windows need never be opened.
Such devices, however, cannot completely mask
the faint human sounds
of the icy wind.

■ GREED SUITE:
JOB CREATION

While you're on shift, a burglar
is breaking into your wallet.
Whether your billfold is tucked
into your back pants pocket
or is inside your purse in the bottom drawer of your desk,
each hour you work
a thief is taking money you earn.
If you suddenly reach out a hand
and grab the arm snaking toward your cash
you'll see that arm is connected to
a three-piece suit
or tailored skirt
rather than to a seedy coat with turned-up collar.
This well-dressed individual removes
without your permission
a sizable portion of the dollars
our efforts at the job are worth.
We say: *the further from production someone is
the more money they make.*
But that cash has to come from someplace.

And if you do seize the fingers clutching what you earn
the face at the end of that arm starts to whine
about how hard *it* works
and so how it *deserves* more of your money.
Yet no one said crime is easy.
And how difficult a criminal act is to commit
is seldom accepted as grounds for acquittal.

This is why when you hear
a businessperson crowing about
the number of jobs that result from an enterprise

you know he or she is actually
justifying a robbery:
all the money he or she is prepared to take
from his or her employees.
Thus, instead of automatically applauding
every time a boss or politician intones the words
providing work,
we have to ask: *what kind of jobs*
will be available? What are the hours, conditions;
how long will this employment last? And most of all:
what happens to the dollars that will be made?
How many go for wages, and exactly how rich
will certain thieves become through this arrangement?

Not that I want to disparage crime,
however. Crooks generate lots of work
for law enforcement agencies
and the manufacturers of each of the fascinating devices
the police purchase annually.
Criminals cause employment for locksmiths,
for the legal profession, courthouse maintenance firms
and the entire prison system
—which involves everything from fencing contractors
to wholesalers of chairs.
Then there are insurance companies
with their agents and inspectors and secretaries.
The person prying open a window in your house
and the person cutting a ribbon to launch a new video store
are both responsible for creating jobs.
What is odd is that one of these individuals
is frequently honored and rewarded by the state
while the other is condemned.
This leads to some contradictions
in official morality: business provides employment
so it's good
whereas crime provides employment
but it's bad.
The real situation, though, is simpler.
At present, work creates crime.
But crime
creates jobs.

■ GREED SUITE:
ATTITUDES AT THE TOP OF A HIERARCHY
INFLUENCE CONDUCT BELOW

The company was going to lay off
one mechanic for a while
because they predicted
a business slowdown.
So Dave called together
ten of the people on his shift: welders like himself
and the other mechanics.
Dave had figured if they each
gave up a day of work every two weeks
that would add up to the hours necessary
to let the mechanic keep his job.
The layoff wouldn't last more than a few months
according to the company, and Dave calculated
when taxes were considered
each of them would be out only thirty-four dollars
over two weeks.

                    ''They wouldn't go for it,''
Dave said. ''The guy who talked loudest
against the idea
was the same old-timer who told me the week before
he has nearly a hundred thousand dollars
in retirement savings plans
and just sold his house in Vancouver
for another hundred thousand.
Yet no way is he going to pass up
thirty-four dollars every couple of weeks.
And he's supposed to be a strong union man.
He did help get a better union
in here a few years ago
and he speaks out at contract time.
But he says if somebody else loses their job
that's just their dumb luck.''

GREED SUITE:
FOLK TUNE

A single guitar chord
vibrates, then pauses.
The human story
is about to begin

accompanied, now, by the soft riffle
of money being counted
in the hum of the life-support machines.

GREED SUITE:
THE PLAGUE
Vancouver

House after house down this avenue:
two-story, wooden, some with a small attic window
under the peak of a steeply-pitched roof.
Lawns. Stairs rising to the porches.
These dwellings seem unchanged
from last month or last year.
There is no evidence of
increased neglect: a drainpipe
now leaning away from the eaves
or a broken pane of glass
freshly patched with cardboard.
Nor are there clues indicating improvements:
a contractor's sign
in the front yard, a neat stack of two-by-fours
beside the walk, or a construction bin at the curb
heaped with broken sheetrock, old piping and sawdust.

But the customary appearance of these homes
hides a corruption
that has transformed them.
They are gripped with a sickness
that spreads along the joists
or the paths of the wiring,
that has leaped from roof to roof

along this block like a fire
that consumes without sound or smoke,
that has gutted these buildings
invisibly.

Without a dollar
being spent on paint
or without a single light bulb being replaced
or even the kitchen linoleum swept,
the houses are now priced
higher than last week,
double what they were worth two years ago.
This afternoon, when one of the dwellings is sold
nobody will hunt down the framers or
heating duct installers
of thirty years before
and place cheques in their surprised hands.
No one will locate the former owners of the building
to share with them the increase in value.
Instead, other women and men
will bank this new wealth
created from nothing, from a bacillus
borne on the air, a tainted spore
that benefits only a
few. And the disease that infects the homes
also afflicts people—everybody who gets to say
when asked to sum up their existence:
"I bought a house. I worked my whole life
to pay for a place to live." Or:
"The new landlord said the rent had to increase that much,
otherwise he couldn't cover his costs."

Those who prosper
from this plague
mainly are immune to its adverse effects
because of a previous exposure
to lesser doses of the illness.
Yet other human beings
who have not developed antibodies
contract the disease from simply handling or coming too near

dollars that carry the germs of this malignancy.
Such men and women exhibit a hectic fever
that leaves them prideful
and haggard, arrogant and crushed
in turn.

The destructive contagion created from air
probably will at last return to the air.
But not before it alters too many lives,
hurts too many people, cripples
the host
on which it grew.

■   GREED SUITE:
    THE SKELETON

Greed has its shadow.
A bloated person gorging
herself or himself
projects behind
the shape of a skeleton.
No matter how furiously
the greedy eat—choking down handfuls of abundance,
sweeping armloads more along the table toward themselves,
the shadow by their chair
remains gaunt.
Flights to sunny beach resorts
across thousands of kilometres of water
cannot shake this companion.
Far below the aircraft, skimming the ocean surface
is the dark outline
of bones.

The shadow is not linked to these men and women
at the soles of their feet. Rather, it begins
at the head.
Thus a skull's
damp, earthen breathing
rhythmically cools the skin of their faces.

Despite living so close to darkness
they insist they do not understand
why they are joined to the grisly being.

But the spectre dims their happiness.
The amount they own does not make them joyous,
at ease, good to others.
All they swallow piles up
as bitter yellow fat
around the heart.
They sometimes boast such plumpness is
insulation from the world.
Yet their possessions do not free them
from wanting more
or from anger at the poor,
at the poor's obstinate hunger.
And to have this frightening silhouette
trail them as if a result of their wealth
they consider
unfair.

■   GREED SUITE:
    THE SALMON
    for Terry Glavin

In October, in the waters of the Gulf
the salmon circle.
More than two million pinks and sockeye
swim in a great turning wheel.
For the first time in memory, the fish have balked
at entering the Fraser River,
the mouth that leads back
to where they were born,
where they would spawn and die
in the tributaries of the Thompson River
and Adams Lake, the Bonaparte and
Nicola watersheds. Biologists in helicopters
and boats
hover over the immense ring
that has appeared off Sand Heads.

These men and women talk of
changes in sea currents
or genetic mutations. But no one is sure if,
instead, the salmon recall
their birth-grounds choked
with stumps and branches, with soil
carried down by the runoff
that is also a consequence of logging.
Or if they remember that the coastal estuaries
where as fingerlings they paused
to acclimatize themselves to ocean
are polluted and blocked.
Or has some chemical trigger
detectable in the fish's brain
informed them that the river
holds less water this season than ever before?
And thus the stone projections
behind which the salmon moving upstream need to rest
are now above the surface
as are the fish-ladders that men constructed
so the salmon could pass the rubble
blasted by the railroad builders into the canyons?

Do the salmon comprehend
the river had to shrink
and spawning creeks be destroyed
because the fiscal year has entered the food chain?
Are they able to understand
it is the dams of the power corporation
that have eaten too much of the water?
Certain authorities could at least
order spillways opened.
In far cities, though, women and men carrying briefcases
battle up the levels of the hierarchy
to find the right office to
spawn paper and words.
These visitors offer presentations
on the economic marginality of commercial fishing
and the importance to the nation
of the financial health of their *own* firms.

So the ministries announce a program
to study the issue.

                    Yet beyond the river delta
salmon continue to arrive from the Pacific
to school together
like an enormous silent protest rally
outside a seat of government.
Occasionally, however,
a thousand or more of the most desperate
spin away from the huge revolving mass
and into the river. For the majority it is futile.
They try to work from pool to pool
over the rocks where the water is shallowest.
Those who succeed must head into the torrents
of the canyons, where the expected stopping places
are gone. The leaps the salmon attempt
up the cataracts
are beyond their endurance. The exhausted fish
are driven downstream.
A few spawn uselessly
along the banks of the lower river
before death.

But always that galaxy of salmon
turns and turns offshore in the salt sky
as if out of this swirling rotation
a thought will take shape and
flash along the neurons,
some action to ensure their survival,
a plan
not yet formed.

■   GREED SUITE:
       THE FALSE SEASON

1.

Day to day, we live in a false season.
The sky overhead, the trees with their changing colors

no less than the downtown streets and
suburban shopping districts
are all projections on a screen.
Summer may be displayed on this curtain
during mid-winter
or autumn may happen on and also
behind the screen. But in the latter case
the two autumns are not alike.

The existence of these images we face, we
live among
is revealed by faulty seams in the curtain.
On a bus, for instance,
the people depicted in the transom ads
and the men and women who ride with you
obviously do not inhabit the same planet.
One of these groups of human beings
is sham.

And the presence of the screen itself
is most evident when women and men, for a time,
stop supporting the curtain
on which a different reality is projected.
This occurs if, together,
we lower a portion of the screen,
that is,
we strike.
Any withdrawal of labor
ruptures for a moment the
three-hundred-and-sixty degree picture
being shown of our world. Through the empty space
where formerly our work maintained the curtain
everyone can now see
an unfamiliar landscape leading into the distance.
The missing part of the screen
is a break in a wall
and the men and women who picket
hold that doorway open.

When a larger section of the barrier that surrounds us

is brought down by
a civic, industry-wide, or even national
general strike,
much more of the Earth's surface
can be viewed. If the strike lasts long enough
we become aware of the real temperature
and wind velocity
prevalent nearby at this time of year.

Walking the line where the curtain
was sustained as though rooted in concrete,
braced by steel,
we can learn from speaking to other people like ourselves
an accurate account of conditions at their jobs,
of their lives, and marvel at
how easily the screen fell.
It is as if we were the first
to step into a garden.
We start to speculate about the territory beyond
and talk of the strange weather.

2.

No wonder our strikes
are greeted with such abhorrence
by those who pay for
the round-the-clock projections.
Whenever a section of screen is lowered
men and women cease watching
the flickering shadows. The projector, also, is
silenced
and in the awkward quiet
we hear sounds previously unattended to
—including each other's voices
now clearer
as when an electronic filter rids music
of machine noise or distortion.

And because we have temporarily refused

to move within a stream of somebody else's visions
we begin to walk differently,
to stand with increased assurance,
to transform ourselves into other than our functions:
producer/consumer/parent/hobby-carpenter.

The more widespread and enduring
any absence of the facade,
the more threatened
the owners of the images become.
So these strikes
must be expunged
from history or memory
and when they recur
must be shattered immediately
or, at worst, explained away.
For if enough of the screen falls
for too lengthy a period
what we have occasion to glimpse
takes years to fade
from the optic nerve
despite frantic and expensive increases
in what is flashed onto the restored screen.

For the owners, a strike is an affront
to the reality they purchase
and thus is a crime
against reality,

that is, against their property,
that is, against
the biological basis of
life. No punishment is too severe
for those who tamper with the curtain.
A prolonged investigation and trial, however,
might remind people of their experiences.
So swift retribution
is best.

3.

Yet because the owners understand
there are flaws in the structure,
they know rebelliousness is bound to appear.
To combat this, an image of a person
is placed at intervals in front of us
and a barrage of figures and words
intends to convince us this picture
represents us,
articulates our hopes, will solve
our complaints.
If we disagree, we are urged to consider
the image of another person
projected before us next.
As with daily television,
the majority of us get to select
from choices others have decided on
and arranged to have created.
A handful of individuals with money
determine the programs available
and how effectively these are realized.
This is their concept of democracy:
us twisting the dial
to pick between the shades of difference
they provide.
The simple motion of your fingers and hand,
the owners insist, is the proper way
for you to shape your existence,
is how change should be made,
is how you can
improve your life.

And except when we act together
we follow the owners' ideas. We keep busy
discussing the events of the projected seasons
as if they were true. For what is behind the screen
frightens some of us
who have struggled so hard to survive here
and sense that other skills may be needed

if the curtain were dismantled forever.

This is the fear of a newborn
who gasps in terror when the umbilical cord
is about to be severed.
The source that has formed this living organism,
the origin of every bit of nourishment she or he has obtained
is being taken away.
Yet this cord is
a fetter
that must be parted
for the child to thrive, to grow,
to become adult

—to pass from shadows
into the difficult light.

■   GREED SUITE:
     REVENGE OF THE FUTURE

1. TRIAL

Before I die, I want to see
those women and men
who were elected to help us and who
wounded us
be brought to trial.

I do not want them charged
for offenses presently covered by statute.
Periodically one is arrested
for lying about campaign contributions or
benefiting financially
from information obtained through their position.
They are convicted
and then let off with the mildest penalty
to demonstrate to the rest of us
the law is equally applied
and to reassure everyone who daily betrays us
their conduct is not so bad.

Instead, I want those chosen to rule us
indicted for crimes against humanity.
In a rich country, these well-off people
knowingly administer to the poor
lethal injections of continuing poverty.
Health or transit services we need
that were established with public money
they grant to their friends
to sell to us. Other community funds
that could ease or enhance our lives
they donate to private enterprises for the profit of a few.
Where there is forest or farmland
they strip it
for conversion to real estate.
New legislation is passed to coerce us
back to the subservience on the job we had overcome to a degree
through years of struggle.
Money is found to outline a city's bridges in lights
but cash is not available to feed the hungry.

To bring the individuals responsible for such policies
into court at last
to face those whose lives were damaged or disrupted
by laws the accused approved
would establish a Nuremberg for social crimes.
No later politician, of whatever doctrine,
would be able to excuse herself or himself
on the grounds of ignorance of their decisions' effects
on other human beings.

And yet
I am aware the officials charged
will be as unrepentant as any concentration camp guard
finally confronted by his aged victims.
The eyes of those who administered us
would display the same irritation
and impatience: *of course I did these things
and I'd do them again.* The accused's statements in court,
icily polite, respect the forces that have brought them here.
They regret only they are now subject to others' will

rather than subjecting men and women to their own.
Everything about them exudes
fear and contempt for the poor,
for the powerless: *I submit myself now*
because you won, you have control.
When I had power, I inflicted what I wanted
on you. At this moment, through some mischance
you have power, so you do the same to me.
Really, we are exactly the same
which makes your talk about justice
the usual farce.

Their belief is that judgment is bought and sold,
that history is written by hired liars,
that dollars and obedience are
the sole measures of responsibility.
Thus they only half-listen
to the months of testimony,
sneering slightly as a witness becomes emotional
at what a regulation meant
when spelled out in human behavior
or as a person shouts their rage
at the waste there was in opposing these officials:
to have to spend our sweet time alive,
our imagination and ingenuity and sweat
to protect ourselves from those we were compelled by law to pay
to devastate our life.

Such witnesses, though,
do not speak to convert the accused
to human solidarity. The intent is to provide
a record, a covenant
to which succeeding women and men
can point as warning
and inspiration: *this must not occur*
again and *this is conduct our species has decided*
is intolerable, is a criminal act
against us all.

2. CORRECTION

But if the jury concludes
an individual is guilty, what punishment
is appropriate?
Can we sentence a person
—as she or he did their fellow citizens—
to a poverty
where each move is monitored by bureaucrats
so the condemned never enjoy themselves
or advance?
Surely we did not break free of a structure
that perpetuates deprivation
in order to inflict it on someone else
—even our enemies?

Should we cage the guilty, as their laws
crammed us into barred rooms
guarded by the stick and the dollar?
Or should they be executed
since it is shown their decrees led
to *our* deaths
from cold and sickness,
malnutrition, alcohol,
heroin?
Yet what would such procedures
tell of our commitment
to treat each other in a new way?

How much pain is fitting
to apply to those who arranged
for us to strangle, year after year,
on gallows they erected from their avarice?
Or, can men and women be rehabilitated
who do not understand
why their actions were wrong?

The wealth they stole—legally or not—
can be reclaimed.
The communities they destroyed can be rebuilt

finer than before.
But we lack the means to completely heal
the lives they tore ajar.
And what can we do with these ex-leaders,
who bear our form and features
yet despise us?

Their greed was the mountain
shadowing all our existences:
a mountain wooded with lies
about how good it was to stay in this shadow,
about how this shadow represented opportunity,
about how evil those of us were
who wanted to clear a road through the trees
that we might journey away from this place
onto an open plain.

     Once we have travelled, however,
     a great distance in the light
     this verdict and punishment must remain visible
     like an obelisk still discernible on the horizon behind
     to mark how far we have come.

Therefore our correction for these guilty
must be our forgiveness.
Despite every urge and instinct
that has kept us, also, vicious and scrabbling
we must counter their selfishness, their meanness
with another part of our humanity.
Let them exist among us, forgiven,
with their sour hearts for companions,
unable, now, to hurt anybody
any more. They will at least know themselves outcast,
poisoned by their own bile,
as though infected by a terminal yet
incommunicable disease.
Let them hear around them our laughter,
more searing than any lash.
Our children growing up free of their vices
will be a daily reproach.

The bright, better world we construct around them
shall be evidence of what they could have been alive for
instead of their plans to seize
and hoard the darkness.

Let our improvement
be their eternal trial

and our revenge.

■ MARSHALL-WELLS ILLUMINATION

■ MARSHALL-WELLS ILLUMINATION
for Jim Daniels

One bright morning, I was sent
to the wholesale cash-and-carry hardware,
glad to be out of the pounding and saws
of the jobsite, to drive the city streets
and walk into the wooden-floored building.

At the counter, the lone clerk
I had spoken with several times before
—an old man, surely past retirement—
fussed at his order books, precise
as his usual shirt and tie
concerning *common* or *finishing,*
galvanized or *not,*
lengths and amounts needed.
The stock numbers were passed
to somebody else for fulfillment
and I stood waiting, in my workclothes and boots.
Motes of dust
rose and drifted in the sunlight
that leaned in from windows down the long room
where a dozen other people toiled at desks.
Then a man entered
from outside, older than me,
younger than the clerk, dressed in coveralls
and leather carpenter's apron.
He pulled a list from a pocket
and stepped aside, as the counter clerk
bent once more to flip the pages of the catalogs
to set the number of each item
on the proper form.

                    And the man in coveralls,
perhaps for pleasure at the new day,
suddenly shifted his heavy boots back and forth
in a clumsy part of a dance
and stopped, grinning.

The motion caught the clerk's eye, and he frowned.
But the man
stomped his boots
in another quick pattern. He paused
under the clerk's dour gaze,
then resumed: the thick soles toeing the planks
and tipping back on heels,
nails falling from the pouches of his apron
as his arms flew out for balance. The man,
laughing, looked over at me for approval.
And the clerk also faced in my direction
shaking his head to invite me to mock
the ridiculous swaying.

                        But at this moment
        I knew
neither gravity nor
centrifugal force
spins the Earth through space.
Our planet revolves
under the dancing feet of this man
and those like him: through their efforts
the immense bulk of our home
is moved. And I understood
as the boots crashed down, this joy
finds even in the dreadful agreements we labor in
the love required to trample
what we have been given
under our invincible shoes.

                        Yet the three of us
hung suspended
in the amber light:
Grandfather Paper and Order,
Father Happiness and Measuring Tape
and myself. The rest of the office watched us
from their file drawers and typewriters
as I saw the planet lurch forward
with each kick of these feet
and the Earth also pushed on

by the weight of an invoice
dropped from an aged hand, saw Father and Grandfather
both turned
to ask me to choose
—one motionless, the other beginning to slow:

what could I do
but dance?

◼ AFTERWORD: WORK, MONEY, AUTHENTICITY

The California poet Lew Welch tells a story to explain his intentions for his poetry. Although Welch's writing is very different from mine, I like what he says:

> Once, on the way to Oregon, I stopped at a California winery to get free wine from the tasting room. Just at that time a tour was starting so I decided to go along. A young man of about 23 was the guide and began that strange kind of language guides use, almost a chant: . . . *and on the left, a 1,500-gallon redwood barrel containing Burgundy kept always at the temperature of.* . . and then he said *Whose kid is that?*
>
> The force of *whose kid is that* caused everyone to pay attention to the real moment we were all in. A small child was about to fall into a very deep vat of wine.
>
> I vowed, at that moment, that every statement in my poems should have at least the force of *whose kid is that.*
>
> It is an impossible standard, but a good one. Few really bad lines can stand against it.

The aim for my own poetry that I take from Welch's anecdote is that I want my writing to assist myself and if possible the reader "to pay attention to the real moment" we are all in. To accomplish this, I want to adopt language that is forceful enough and authentic enough to clearly and convincingly depict what is happening to us and around us.

1. The Real Moment

How then do I see the real moment we are in? At the center of our lives, and so of my aesthetic, I see the overwhelming majority of us going to work each day, and I see how the work we do profoundly influences nearly every aspect of our time alive. Where we live, how well we live, how much free time we have, how much mental and physical energy we have when off work, are all a consequence of the jobs we have or of our search for employment. Our attitudes to nearly every aspect of our existence, including to those traditional subjects of English-language poetry—love, death and nature, are also enormously influenced by the kind of work we do. Who our friends are, what

116

our response is to how society uses the material and natural objects of this planet, and much, much more are all affected in a major way by our employment or lack of it.

And yet, as I have written about elsewhere at length, in our culture there is an almost pathological aversion to presenting an accurate portrayal of daily work. Whether you flip around the television dial, scan the shelves of a bookstore, or attend a ballet or play, an accurate assessment of what it like for us to go to work is a taboo subject.

I remember a couple of years ago strolling up and down the aisles of publishers' displays at the Canadian Booksellers Association annual convention. There were books on every conceivable subject, from butterflies to biographies of film stars, from Thai cooking to Egyptian rugs. But *entirely* missing was any book on the central and governing daily experience of most Canadians—the work we have to do.

This taboo exists not only in the entertainment and cultural sectors of our society, but in our educational institutions as well. And this taboo is not just an interesting anthropological fact; it hurts people. Some years ago I was giving a reading of my poems in a first-year sociology class at the University of Windsor. The instructor there told me his first assignment for the students is to have them interview in depth a person who is employed at the job they ultimately want to have after graduation.

The instructor reported the results are dramatic. Students drop out of the class, quit university, change majors. The instructor pointed out that the students were willing to launch themselves into four years of expensive study toward a goal about which they had only the haziest conception.

As a teacher now myself, I can verify that this situation continues. I asked a composition class I taught recently, made up of accounting students, how many of them had ever sat down and talked in detail to an accountant about his or her work before committing themselves to years of preparation for this occupation. Half the class raised their hands, leaving half the class admitting that they had no accurate knowledge of what employment as an accountant is really like.

A glance at high school curriculums demonstrates how rooted the taboo is. We insist our students know many facts about geography, mathematics, languages. But the students leave school more or less completely ignorant of their legal rights at work—overtime and holiday pay, for instance. They leave school equally ignorant of how to qualify for work-related social programs such as unemployment insurance, workers' compensation, welfare. Like the confusion over a choice of occupation, this lack of knowledge about the history or present status of these rights and programs tangibly *hurts* our young people once they enter the workforce. The taboo results in men and women striving to attain a job for which they may discover they are temperamentally not suited. And the taboo means young people unaware of labour law frequently fall prey to unscrupulous employers.

Personally, I find it discouraging that the literary arts—which are touted (and funded) as epitomizing the human spirit—should help perpetuate the taboo against accurately depicting daily work and thus contribute to human pain. I find offensive each new anthology of Canadian poetry, prose or drama that once again offers a literary portrait of a country—in which *nobody works.* For as the feminist authors and the writers from minority communities have shown, by what we teach (or write or read), we teach (or create or learn) a theory of value. When we omit the experience of women, for instance, we teach something of the value of that experience. When we omit the experience of daily work, we teach something of the value of that experience. Our entire society functions, however, only because each of us reconstructs the world through our daily repetitive tasks. To cloak this fact in a taboo conceals the central contribution our lives make to the larger community, and so hampers a full understanding both of our community and of our individual lives.

I believe the *reason* for the taboo becomes evident once the taboo is broken and we look honestly at what happens to us at the job. For it is evident we are not free, there. The workplace remains a portion of our lives where we do not yet enjoy the democracy we are told is our birthright—off the job. Hence we live in a daily absurdity. Off work we are assured we are responsible citizens whose vote determines the direction of the nation. But once we show up at work, we are informed that the money the owners' possess (or the political power some Party possesses) unquestionably entitles them to give us orders which we must obey. We are directed to accept the present structure of authority at work as a fact of nature, just as at one time the divine right of kings to rule us was regarded as undebatable, indeed, natural.

Here again the taboo against an accurate depiction of daily work *hurts* people. Most of us have to some degree chafed at the grotesque aspects of the perpetuation of undemocratic workplaces in a supposedly democratic society. But the taboo keeps us isolated in our response, since if we don't read or hear these matters discussed we're not sure if we're the only people to feel exactly as we do. And the silence on this subject also gives us no opportunity to respond to other people's opinions, that is, to think critically about what is happening to us at the job. The taboo hence limits our understanding of what occurs at work, and impedes our chances of arriving at a collective means of altering our situation for the better.

I stress the phrase "*accurate* depiction of daily work" when considering the taboo because a romanticized or sanitized portrayal of the work experience in no way breaks the taboo. Television serials that pretend to show police work or hospital work (*Hill Street Blues, Miami Vice, St. Elsewhere*) are merely the contemporary North American mirror image of Eastern-bloc-style "socialist realism" (which aims to present workers as heroic, rather than to let us articulate the concrete conditions under which we work and hence live). Both sorts of responses to employment present false views of what it is like to work at the jobs depicted (as can be verified by speaking to any actual human being employed in workplaces similar to those shown). And the taboo hides other similarities between East and West. For instance, both North American "right-wingers" and Russian or, say, Polish Communist Party members endorse an *identical* program when it comes to labour. Strangely enough, both believe in a ban on strikes, in requiring any unions that exist to be government-approved, and that unions and management should work together to maximize production while minimizing costs. It is this demonstrated unity of purpose with regard to working people that has led me to abandon the left/right split as a way of looking at politics. For me, a more accurate scheme for classifying where people stand is to regard them as anti-authoritarian or authoritarian. Does someone believe working people should have

119

the same right to democracy at work as they do off the job? Or, does someone produce ''reasons'' (or worse) to insist the workplace must always remain undemocratic in structure?

The real moment we are all in, then, is for me an historical time when everywhere on the planet the majority of people—those of us who are employed for a living—have not yet attained democracy at work. We are not free women and men during the major part of our waking life. But the real moment I am in also includes living in a particular corner of North America where certain horrid economic and social concepts have been adopted by the regional authorities.

Since 1983, British Columbia's government has put into practice a number of attitudes toward people that have come to be associated with, for instance, prime minister Margaret Thatcher of England and to a lesser extent former president Ronald Reagan of the USA. In some areas of implementing this philosophy, the BC government even has been an innovator, as our local politicians like to boast. At the heart of these policies is the idea that the only measure of value is money. The good of the whole community, or of the environment, or of the future are nothing compared to the opportunity for a handful of individuals to make the largest possible immediate profit out of what were formerly considered public resources or public services.

The adoption of the dollar as the sole measure of value carries with it an enormous social cost. ''Ice in the veins means money in the bank,'' is the slogan, for example, found on some Vancouver licence plate holders. Meanness, here, is considered a virtue: first publicly (in decrees slashing every form of government help for our neighbors in need), then privately (in interpersonal relations at every level). And the widening gap between the rich and the majority is encouraged. After all, people who possess money must by *definition* possess virtue if money is the only measure of value. And by the same standard, those people with less money must be worth less. So my city has seen the simultaneous appearance of soaring real estate prices, a multiplying of expensive boutiques offering luxury goods, and ever-lengthening Food Bank lines.

In carrying out its political program, the BC government has, as mentioned, drastically reduced every type of social service— from educational opportunities to welfare rates. The public money thus freed for other use has been poured into a series of financially-disastrous megaprojects: a huge coal development in the Northeast of the province, at a time when the Southeastern coal fields could not sell their product; a world exposition; a highway that duplicates existing routes into the province's Interior and ended up costing a billion dollars. Each project enriched a tiny number of well-connected people at the expense of the majority. Official rates of unemployment here now stand one-and-a-half times as high as the national average, since the social services cut were labour intensive, and the megaprojects chosen are not.

Thus, for years myself and my friends have lived in a region where the government has exhibited a more-than-usually-fervent belief that the purpose of social organization is to reward an already-affluent minority at the expense of the majority. One consequence has been the growth of individual rage, as some service formerly available—for the elderly, for the desperately sick, for children—is no longer present when you need it. In frustration, you begin to dream of blowing the head off some functionary of the ruling party with a high-powered rifle and of the satisfaction in lashing out at last in some such way. But then you quickly realize this is the dream of Northern Ireland, this is the dream of Beirut. So for now the anger gets channelled towards your immediate family and friends or drowned in chemical stimulants and depressants or sucked in deep and held, burning.

In 1983 the entire province fought back, with an escalating public sector general strike backed by a myriad of community groups appalled by the destruction of community wealth and community opportunity. But this strike was cruelly betrayed at the height of its success by a trade union leadership that had become terrified of what success would mean, terrified of the depth and breadth of discussion and argument that had arisen to re-examine every social institution. And the betrayal, coming as it did so near to victory, taught the population the futility of opposition. Cynicism, black humor, numb endurance became the mood of the resistance. The trade union leadership received their reward from the government in the form of a new series of violently anti-labour laws. In response, in 1987 a one-day provincial general strike was called. But the labour leadership was extremely wary this time of rousing popular support. The protest

strike was kept completely isolated from community participa –
tion, and rigidly limited to one day only. Though all sectors of the
trade union movement did shut down for the day, the mood on
the picket lines was vastly different than 1983. Everyone in 1987
knew the action was a farce, a gesture. This was not combat, not a
fight to win.

As for a political opposition, that effectively disappeared in
1983. The opposition parties, as frightened of community
extra-parliamentary activity as the ruling party, patiently explain
to anyone who will listen that all action is futile except electing
them. They preach the gospel of humble suffering until the time
rolls around when you get the chance to send to the well-paid
legislature the men and women their party has selected to
"represent" you. Meanwhile, they do their best to assure
businessmen and women—local, national and international—that
they, too, hold money sacred. While they promise to restore
social programs to a degree, they also strive to convince the
commercial world of the immediate, dollars-and-cents benefits to
business of such a program.

So this is the real moment out of which the poems in this
collection arise, and to which they intend to draw attention. Not
every poem here is directly concerned with daily work, of course,
or with life under the rule of money. But this is the context in
which the book's author views love, death, nature, or any other
topic found in its pages.

2. Using Language

Yet this is a book of poems. The writing here does not seek to call
attention to the moment we are all in by means of prose like this
afterword, or prose such as magazine or newspaper journalism, or
prose fiction. I believe contemporary poetry provides the best
medium for articulating what is happening to us. Here's what
Lew Welch says about the possibilities for poetry:

> The guide in the winery, at the moment he said *Whose
> kid is that,* was using language in an exact relationship with
> his consciousness. He was trying to get some work done . . .
> And the people on the tour responded immediately . . . The
> child, thereby, was saved.

Poetry should be at least as intense as this. It very seldom is.

The few poems we prize over the centuries and across all cultures and times are *more* intense than this.

The way I am ''using language'' in this collection (with what I hope is the intensity Welch calls for) utilizes that form of imaginative writing we call contemporary poetry. To me, poetry's directness, its comparative brevity, enable a writer to use language ''in an exact relationship'' with consciousness better than does prose. However, most people's introduction to poetry as a toddler or in school leaves them with the conviction that poetry is distinguished from prose not by the qualities Welch praises but by the adoption of a regular pattern of recurring sounds at the end of lines (rhyme) and a regular pattern of recurring beats in those lines (metre). Beginning at the turn of the last century, though, poets began to move away from such patterns. The poets felt these regular forms imply that the world depicted by the poem is as neat, tidy, predictable as the patterns. And the Twentieth Century has proven to be anything but neat, tidy, predictable. So instead of rhyme and metre, poets began to convey what they have to say using careful selection of words (for instance, choosing conventional, rather than ''poetic,'' diction and word order). Poets also pay careful attention to rhythms (where emphasis falls in conversational speech, for example) and to the creation of original forms through which to present their material (variable line breaks, for instance, so that line length differs within each poem).

This change in what constitutes poetry has left many people unsure how to evaluate the worth of contemporary poems. Now, in an era when novelty is prized, when change is the norm, value in the arts is often linked to the *new*. For much of this century we have expected to find the new in experiments with form. Pound, Eliot, H.D., Stein, Thomas and a host of other writers were regarded by their peers as breaking new ground because of their manipulation of literary forms. This definition of the new remains current, and has parallels in the fine arts, music, dance and many other components of our artistic life.

But alterations in form do not represent the only possible aspect of the new. In the long history of English-language poetry, fiction and drama there have been moments and periods in which the new is manifest as a major shift in content. The writings of the Romantics at the start of the Nineteenth Century are one example of this. The poems of Blake, Wordsworth, Keats, Shelley are not very different formally than those of the writers considered mainstream at the time the Romantics began to express their horrified response to the industrial revolution. Yet the subject matter and tone and attitudes of the Romantics constitute a pronounced change in the course of English-language literature. Ironically, nearly two hundred years later most people equate "poetic" with "Romantic." But in their own day the Romantic poets were seen as being so new they were regarded as the antithesis of "real" poets like Milton or Pope.

What I see as new in my poems is not experiments in poetic form but in content. Form here reproduces free verse techniques that by now are rather standard; I find these forms effective as a means of expression. The new factor here is the pervasive consciousness that the conditions of daily work in our time is what shapes the world. This poetry is thus other than a "spontaneous overflow of powerful feelings," as Wordsworth called it. And this poetry also rejects the concept of art as a means to escape from the everyday. Such an escape, after all, is bogus; the reader must return to the life from which he or she wished to flee. And nothing in such art provides any insights as to the causes of the reader's unhappiness with her or his present existence, nor any discussion of possible means to improve that existence. Like any narcotic, such art merely dangles an unattainable illusion of a happier life before a person who wants something better in the real world.

Instead of these possibilities for poetry, the new poetry I am interested in writing becomes a place where *ideas*, as well as feelings, can be articulated, argued, defended. Thus this writing combines an emphasis on feelings with an older notion of poetry that includes narrative, advocacy, debate—a concept of poetry familiar to the Augustan era and to Milton, for instance.

But such a new task for poetry necessarily proposes different virtues for the genre than previously were accepted as the norm. It often appears to me that what is praised in contemporary poetry is the clever way an author can cover up banal ideas by means of his or her skill at word choice or at inventing novel poetic forms.

The new poetry of which my writing aims to be part instead selects as its principal virtue authenticity. This choice makes sense to me, since I believe the most important function of art is to illuminate our current situation so that we may ponder the next steps the human race can take to improve our common lot. And if we are to consider how to alter the world for the better, we surely must start from an unflinchingly honest portrayal of how the world is now.

We know from Einstein, though, that any observation of a phenomenon affects the phenomenon being observed. I believe to fully understand some aspect of our life we have to isolate it for detailed study and meditation, but also we have to observe the way it functions when meshed with the rest of the universe. Hence these poems rely often on metaphor, at times extended metaphor. Something in the world is described here in terms of another thing, in the hope this will remove the primary subject of the poem from its familiar context and allow the writer (and reader) to better examine and comprehend the primary subject. As the metaphor is extended, the intention is to learn more about how the primary subject functions under a number of circumstances. We also are aware from our experiences of ordinary conversation that such use of metaphor can create the intense use of language demanded for poetry by Welch in his quote above.

A recurring metaphor of the present collection is sociosomatic illnesses—how daily life in hierarchically-organized enterprises and institutions negatively affects the human organism. One important means we have of coping with such daily existence is humor, however. So a number of poems here employ humor in considering their subject. Although we're taught that a serious approach to reality has more value than a comic one, in my experience seriousness is neither the sole nor the most effective attitude people adopt in order to deal with the joys and sorrows of being alive. I've often felt that our civilization would be a much more pleasant one if Jesus and Marx, for instance, had cracked a few good jokes in expounding their points of view. What if one of the Parables had been a real rib-tickler? Or if Marx had conveyed some of his points through humor as well as dour earnestness? Would the human race have escaped the horrors of the Inquisition, ''Christian'' civil wars or Leninism? For there is something inhuman about doctrines that take themselves completely seriously. And such inhumanity appears to result in inhuman behavior on the part of advocates of such doctrines. To me, humor must be part of any realistic description or assessment of the human condition, and so it has value equal to seriousness as a means of conveying information about and to humanity.

3. A Small House on the Outskirts of Heaven

This collection begins with a section, "Testimonies," that gathers poems based on descriptions by others and myself of facets of our present working lives. One poem here, "A Cursing Poem," was originally part of a manuscript of my poems eventually issued by Macmillan of Canada in 1974. Because Macmillan felt the poem might be libelous, the poem was dropped from the manuscript before publication. The person who is the target of the poem's anger, Gordon Shrum, died in 1985, however. And since the dead cannot be libeled, this is the first chance the poem has had to appear in a collection of mine (although the poem was published in magazines in both the US and England, and I have often performed it at public readings).

The cursing poem is one of a number of intriguing types listed in Jerome Rothenberg's *Technicians of the Sacred*, an anthology of aboriginal poetries from around the world. But the effectiveness of cursing poetry in our culture—or at least of my attempt at this kind of poem—may be gauged by the fact that although the poem was written in 1971 Shrum did not die until fourteen years later. Indeed, his life in the meantime included such incidents as drinking a beaker of defoliant at a press conference. He did this to refute environmentalists' concern that his company's use of such chemicals on their power line right-of-ways is harmful to the biosphere.

Because the poem was written so long ago, I should comment on the numbers that appear in the poem. At the time the poem was written, the minimum wage was $2 an hour in BC and it cost 25 cents to ride public transit each way. Today the minimum wage is $4.50, two-and-a-quarter times what it was then, but it costs $1.25 to ride the bus—*five* times the 1971 fare. The reference to temperature being 40 degrees refers to Fahrenheit, which was the scale in use in BC in 1971.

The second section, "Local Traffic," combines poems arising from travel with poems about being at home. The latter include pieces concerned with our—and my—present condition.

"Enigmas," the third section, contains poems that as near as I can tell are about failure (as the first poem in the section suggests). These are the poems I understand least in the collection. The next section, "A Yellow Cottage," is an elegy.

The fifth section, "Defective Parts of Speech," groups poems concerned with the misuse of language in our society. The intense use of language that Welch advocates for poetry unfortunately is also achieved at times by advertisers, the news media, politicians and other authority figures—and not usually for our benefit.

"Lost and Found," the next section, gathers some found poems . . . just for fun. "Greed Suite," the following section, explores a number of ways human lives and the natural environment are affected by the ideology that puts money above all other considerations.

Finally, "Marshall-Wells Illumination" attempts to answer through poetry the question sometimes put to me: why do you choose to write about daily work in *poems?* Marshall-Wells was a chain of hardware stores in business across Western Canada.

■ ACKNOWLEDGEMENTS

I very much appreciate the hospitality shown to my words by editors of the magazines that have published, or accepted for publication, most of the poems collected here:

USA: *5 AM, Kayak, The Little Magazine, The Massachusetts Review, The Minnesota Review, North Dakota Quarterly, The Ontario Review, Poetry Northwest, Processed World, Radical America.* "Birds, in the Last of the Dark," "Economic Meditations," "The Emptiness of Business," and "A Yellow Cottage" first appeared in *The Hudson Review.* "In a Small House on the Outskirts of Heaven" first appeared in *TriQuarterly*, a publication of Northwestern University.

Canada: *Canadian Dimension, Canadian Forum, Canadian Literature, Cross-Canada Writers' Quarterly, Don't Quit Yr Day-Job, Event, Fiddlehead, Labour* (special issue of *Athabasca University Magazine*), *Malahat Review, New Directions, New Quarterly, Outlook, Poetry Canada Review, Prism International, Quarry, Taproot, University of Windsor Review.*

Other: *Fireweed* (England), *Meanjin* (Australia)

I am also grateful for a Canada Council Arts Grant in 1985 – 86 which gave me time for some of these poems. The quotations from Lew Welch in the afterword are from the essay "Language Is Speech" in his *How I Work as a Poet* (Bolinas, CA: Grey Fox Press, 1973). This collection is in memory of Dr. G.J. (Jack) Millar. And it is

for Dave Bostock and Sandra Nichol